Dancing

THROUGH LIFE

St. Martin's Press ✺ New York

Dancing

THROUGH LIFE

Lessons Learned

on and off the Dance Floor

Antoinette Benevento

with EDWIN DOBB

www.stmartins.com

Design by Maggie Goodman

Library of Congress Cataloging-in-Publication Data

Benevento, Antoinette.
    Dancing through life : lessons learned on and off the dance floor / Antoinette Benevento with Edwin Dobb.
        p. cm.
    ISBN-13: 978-0-312-37085-5
    ISBN-10: 0-312-37085-7
    1. Conduct of life. 2. Dance—Miscellanea. 3. Dance—Philosophy. I. Dobb, Edwin, 1950– II. Title.

BJ1595.B456 2007
158.1—dc22

                                                                    2007019469

First Edition: September 2007

10 9 8 7 6 5 4 3 2 1

To my parents, Tony and Helen Dobb,
who were beside me every step of the way,
cheering me on, helping me back to my feet
when I stumbled, inspiring me through their quiet
strength, faith in life, and love for each other

Contents

CONTENTS

Acknowledgments

Years ago, when I was single, as well as single-minded about dance, I returned often to my hometown, Butte, Montana. One of my favorite rituals during those visits was to engage in some form of outdoor physical activity with my brother, Edwin Dobb, who had moved back to Butte after working first as a magazine editor and then an independent writer in New York. While hiking or inline skating, Ed and I would talk about everything under the sun. Movement stimulated conversation. At the time, I owned and operated several Fred Astaire dance studios in the Phoenix area. The well-being of those studios, and the managers and instructors who staffed them, was always on my mind. So it was no surprise when one day, while we were skating, I found myself yet again talking about the challenges of running a business that was growing larger and more complex by the day. I was explaining some of my management strategies in a pretty animated way, when Ed turned to me and said, "You should write a book."

I can't recall how I responded, probably because the notion

both excited and frightened me so much that I was at a loss for words. I knew that the approach I'd developed, a marriage of self-help ideas and dancing principles, was relevant to life away from the dance floor. It had never occurred to me to organize it into a system and present it to the public. My strengths, of course, were dancing and running a dance business, not writing. If there were any writing to be done, someone else would have to do it. The most likely candidate was the guy rolling along next to me. By the time Ed and I finished skating that afternoon, a collaboration had been born. Personal experiences, including the deaths of our father, brother, and brother-in-law in quick succession, and the need to make a living, slowed the development of the proposal. In the process, the basic vision matured and both of us changed in significant ways. We created our own dance, traveling together to emotional and intellectual places we couldn't have reached alone, which was in keeping with the central concept of the book—that we are our relationships. And for that once-in-a-lifetime shared experience, as well as the book that came out of it, I'll always be grateful to my brother. I know he feels the same way, because he's told me so.

Writing a manuscript, no matter how worthy or well done, is no guarantee that anyone will ever read it. We could have published it ourselves, which self-help writers often do. But Ed and I were determined to sign with a major house, to provide the best possible platform for getting the book before a wide audience. The first step toward achieving that was to find an agent who possessed the needed expertise and could appreciate what we were trying to do. Mollie Glick met both requirements, and then some. Her enthusiasm, loyalty, hands-on manner, and wise counsel were invaluable to our securing a contract and delivering the book. Thank you, Mollie.

We are also grateful to Diane Reverand, a widely respected editor with a long and impressive record who recognized the uniqueness of *Dancing Through Life*. She grasped immediately that we had envisioned something more philosophically sophisticated, and thus potentially more enduring, than the run-of-the-mill self-help book. Diane left St. Martin's Press shortly after she acquired the book, but we will always be in her debt for championing our cause. Inheriting another editor's literary child is becoming increasingly common in the publishing world, but that doesn't make it any easier or more welcome. Ed and I were very lucky indeed when St. Martin's chose Nichole Argyres to take on our temporarily orphaned book. More than anyone else, Nichole is the person on the editorial side of the equation who helped bring the project to fruition. And she did so under trying circumstances, including a wickedly short deadline and a couple of last-minute crises. Nichole's assistant, Kylah McNeill, was also instrumental in shepherding the manuscript through to completion, and just in time to meet the original publication date. To Nichole, Kylah, and everyone else at St. Martin's: You're a class act. We couldn't have collaborated with a more talented, conscientious, and dedicated group of people.

Long before there was a book that uses dance as a metaphor for life there was a life of dance, the life that began more than 25 years ago, when I walked into a Fred Astaire dance studio in Reno. Over the course of that life, I've benefited immeasurably from my relationships with dancers, dance partners, managers, instructors, and students. Without them and all that they taught me, *Dancing Through Life* would not exist. I'm especially indebted to my competition partner, Michael Bickley, whose unshakeable faith in us made me believe that he and I could be ballroom champions. We did it, Michael, and in so doing, we created some of the most gratifying dance moments I've ever experienced. I also wish to single out Jack Rothweiler, President and CEO of Fred Astaire Dance Studios, Inc. (FADS). Jack is a man of uncommon energy and conviction who has altered the dance industry forever by opening its doors to many more people and forming synergistic partnerships that extend the reach of FADS. By his example—how he works with others, solves problems, takes advantage of opportunities, and remains true to his vision—Jack has shown me what creative leadership really means. He's also a dear friend, for which I'm also deeply grateful.

Speaking of those close to me: In all that I do, in all that I may ever do or be, my everyday inspiration comes from God's precious gifts—Gage, Jacob, Aspen, Gianna—and their father, my husband, Keith Benevento. During both competitions and exhibitions, Michael Bickley and I often performed a special number that was choreographed to the tune "The Story of My Life" by Neil Diamond. "The story of my life" the first line of the song says, "begins and ends with you." What had once been a signature dance now signifies what Keith means to me. My life today begins and ends with him.

ONE

Prelude: The Art of Balance

I could have danced all night
—LERNER & LOEWE

My life in dance began with a wrong turn—a misstep. It was 1980. I was a freshman studying elementary education at Montana State University in Bozeman, and I was restless. I also was fed up with winter. So I transferred to the University of Nevada, Reno, where I naively imagined I'd escape the snow and subfreezing temperatures that grip my home state from November through March—or April, or even May sometimes. Boy, was I wrong. Reno may be located in a desert, but it's a high, northern desert that's invaded by bone-chilling weather every year.

There I was in one of the country's premier

gambling meccas, where hope not only springs eternal but fills casino coffers around-the-clock, a little wiser geographically certainly but with little reason to be optimistic about *my* ill-advised wager. What in the world had I gained by coming to Reno? Every morning I shivered as I climbed into my car to drive to school and I continued to shiver, and grumbled to myself, as I reported to my job—working the counter at a busy Wendy's. To make matters worse, I registered too late to get the classes I wanted at the university. I now could look forward to at least several months of boredom. And I can't stand boredom.

That's when my fortunes changed forever. Out of the blue, my roommate's boyfriend told me that he was going to try out for an instructor trainee program at the local Fred Astaire Dance Studio. Would I like to be his partner? The idea wasn't entirely foreign, to say the least. From seventh grade through my senior year in high school, I had been a member of school drill teams. I liked to dance, liked it very much. For my last birthday at home, my mother ordered a cake with the following words on top: "The dancing machine is now 18." So after a little hesitation, I applied and was accepted. Within two weeks I had quit the fast food business and shelved my educational plans. I was spending fourteen to sixteen hours at the studio every day of the week, and I danced virtually all of that time. I talked dance, I dreamed dance, I was possessed by dance.

Why? The full answer would require me to tell you everything that's happened since then, and I'll eventually get to the highlights in the chapters to follow. But for now suffice it to say that certain features of dance captivated me from the start.

> *The dance floor is a fantasyland where everyone lives happily ever after.*

Looking back, I realize that something important was missing in my life then. I knew that much. I was searching, but I wasn't sure what I was searching for—until I joined Fred Astaire and began dancing full-time. Suddenly I felt energized, fulfilled. I knew instantly that dancing would become my life. What I'm about to say may strike you as corny but it's the truth: The first time my instructor took me in his arms and swept me across the dance floor, I felt like I was being transported back in time or to another world, a world of elegant balls and fairy-tale romance. The dance floor, I soon learned, was a fantasyland where everyone lives happily ever after. It's a place that stands apart from the everyday world—its conflicts, cruelties, and disappointments. No wonder I became addicted, as do so many others who make the same discovery.

As you might imagine, my job as dance instructor didn't seem like work at all. I was getting paid to impart something I loved to students, which gave me a great deal of pleasure. But I wanted more. I wanted a serious, long-term partner with whom I could practice, someone who would challenge me to improve my skills. That's when the fates placed another opportunity in front of me. A visiting dance coach was impressed by the enthusiasm that I and two other instructors exhibited and suggested we attend a national contest in Miami—as observers, not participants. It would be an opportunity to see how our skills compared with those of the best professional dancers in the Fred Astaire system. Should we find competition appealing, it would also give us a chance to meet potential partners. And we'd be staying in sunny southern Florida, a place I was absolutely certain was warmer than both Montana and Nevada. In my mind I was on my way long before I boarded the plane. Simply stated, I was thrilled.

Thrilled but unprepared for what was about to happen. In Florida, Larry, a young and eager instructor from the Fred Astaire Dance Studio in Phoenix, introduced himself. He explained that he'd been stood up by his partner and was looking for a way to salvage the situation. Then he asked me to dance with him in the novice division. There was no time to get to know each other. Certainly no time for rehearsal. Just step out on the floor and follow his lead. And those were not the only reasons for turning down Larry's proposal. At the time in October 1982, I was ten to fifteen pounds overweight. I lacked proper dance shoes, to say nothing of a traditional dance costume. And if you've ever seen the extravagant outfits contestants wear at professional ballroom dancing events, you can imagine how much like an awkward, out-of-place bird I felt at the time—a drab starling among brightly colored peacocks. Still, against all odds, I found myself saying yes.

Remember the first time you appeared in front of an audience? Now imagine doing so with a stranger and without knowing what exactly you're going to perform. I began wishing I'd never left Nevada. Then I received another sign that dancing would be my destiny. Larry had chosen a rumba, and the moment the music started I was at one with the infectious rhythm of that Latin classic. Instinct guided me as I swam in a sea of sensation—Larry and I turning together across the dance floor, hundreds of eyes watching our every move, and, finally, applause. Real applause. The clapping startled me. We'd certainly won the approval of the audience, but what about the judges? After a short deliberation, they awarded us first place. No one was more surprised than I. I'd come to watch and ended up winning. More important, an ugly duckling had been transformed, if only for a moment, into the belle of the ball.

The following summer I transferred to the Phoenix studio to be able to train with Larry. Our choreographer was a veteran dancer named Michael Bickley. One day Michael asked me to join him in a back room of the studio. "I want to show you something." He placed one hand under my left arm and the other under my right leg, then lifted me in a single, swift movement over his head, just as I'd seen ice dancers do. One moment I'd been standing on the floor, the next I was suspended in the air—and, it seemed, soaring. After work I called my mother to tell her about experiencing for the first time what ballroom dancers call a full press lift. "I felt like I was in a dream," I said excitedly, unsure of what exactly I meant other than that the exhilaration had convinced me that anything's possible. And in that spirit I told her with complete conviction that I was going to become a champion ballroom dancer.

Soon afterward, Michael became my partner and for the next ten years I devoted myself to competition. In 1984 we placed fifth in the World Theatrical Championships. Two years later, we won in the Rising Star Division at the American Smooth Ballroom Championships. When I retired in 1993, we held fifth place overall in the American Smooth. At the same time, I had been moving up the management ladder at the Phoenix studio—from instructor to assistant supervisor to supervisor to assistant manager to manager. The same year I left competition I purchased the studio. That, too, was a turning point in my life, more momentous than any previous, though at the time I couldn't have dreamed of the changes it would bring, including all that led to the writing of this book. From the day I graduated to supervisor I had been a hands-on, face-to-face problem solver. I found great satisfaction in helping staff members resolve differences, overcome obstacles, and communicate more effectively. To better prepare myself for the job, I attended educational seminars. In a sense, I suppose, I was fulfilling the ambition that had initially driven me to become an educator, someone who teaches and counsels. I've always wanted to help others.

But back in the early 1990s I was woefully naïve (as were many of the self-help manuals I looked to for guidance). I grew up thinking that I had to make sure everyone around me was okay, that it was my responsibility to do so. What's more, I fully believed—at least until my early thirties—that there's no reason why everybody shouldn't be okay. In other words, all problems are fixable, provided one brings the right attitude and sufficient commitment to the task. And I was convinced I possessed both. Oh, I had been tested in this belief, having experienced disappointment in love and financial difficulties, the troubles we all hold in common. But the flaw in my outlook wasn't revealed to me until my mother died in 1995. Later I'll say more about the special relationship I enjoyed with Mom and how her loss has affected me. What I wish to convey now is how the incident altered my behavior at the dance studio. Although it may seem so obvious that it doesn't warrant mentioning, I'm convinced it's important to acknowledge out loud and in the presence of others what death teaches us: Some problems aren't fixable and some things aren't knowable. There are strict limits to what we can do and comprehend. Certain things simply aren't possible. Stopping people from dying is one of those things.

Most people who suffer the loss of a loved one are overcome by an urge to cling to life, to make the best of the opportunities at hand. In my case, I found myself looking at the people I worked with in a new light. During those early years of ownership, I was at the studio virtually all of my waking hours, teaching students, training instructors, developing ways to attract new customers, all in an attempt to keep a very promising business growing. Why, I asked myself, when life is so short and unpredictable, should I settle for anything but the most constructive relationships with those who occupy so much of my time? That they happened to be my employees made no difference. Wherever I was, I wanted likable, creative, supportive people around me.

I decided it was time to hold a meeting, the first of my many "Come to Jesus" meetings, and by that I don't mean that I asked my staff to convert to a religious doctrine but rather exposed them to religious-like enthusiasm. I told my staff that I was about to implement a new management philosophy at the studio. I insisted that they abide by what I call the Dance Floor Rules: You must be nice. You must share. You must work together. And most important, you must want to grow up—to mature as a human being. After describing the work environment I envisioned, I tried to demonstrate how that environment would lead to financial success as well as personal fulfillment. To tell the truth, for all my hellfire rhetoric, I wasn't sure back then exactly how we were going to get where I wanted to go. But I saw the destination. And I was determined.

For the next several years I treated the dance studio as a laboratory of human behavior. Like other people in the arts, dancers tend to be more demonstrative than, say, stockbrokers or accountants or auto mechanics. But, appearances aside, they're like everyone else, trying to make sense of their lives, searching for pleasure and companionship, hoping that who they are and what they do will be valued by some and loved by at least a few and, of course, doing what they deem necessary to survive. Much of what I learned about personal growth in that setting echoed what one routinely finds in standard texts of the self-help movement. But to my great delight, the most useful lessons didn't come from observing ordinary behavior. They came from watching people on the dance floor. Ironically, what I'd once seen as a fantasyland started to teach me about reality.

Dance floor rules: You must be nice. You must share. You must work together. You must want to grow up.

I'm certainly not the first person to use dance as a metaphor for life. Nor will I be the last. But what has struck me—and inspired me to write this book—is the thoroughness with which the terms, principles, and techniques of dance can be applied to everyday situations all of us face. Maybe we shouldn't be

> *We are our relationships.*

surprised that an activity as old as human culture, dating back at least thousands of years and probably much longer, should so closely reflect what it means to be human. Consider two of the most fundamental elements of dance—movement and relationship. What is existence but movement and relationship? We live within a complex, continually shifting web of relationships involving family, friends, various social groups, and society as a whole, to say nothing of other organisms, places, ideas, events, and everything that makes up the contemporary world. In the absence of those relationships we could no more exist than a tree could live apart from the ecosystem it depends upon for sustenance. Although people often downplay or misunderstand this fact: *we are our relationships.*

But as everyone knows from experience, not all personal and social relationships are healthy; many are downright harmful, others crippling, some fatal. And precisely to the extent that our relationships are unhealthy, so are we. At this point we could quibble over the chicken-and-egg dilemma of whether we should focus our attention on the individual or the relationship. Is there something wrong with me (or you)? Or is it just that the chemistry is off? Traditionally, psychologists train their sights on the former, looking for causes *within* people, whereas sociologists concentrate on social contexts—external causes, such as one's socioeconomic situation—in their search for the factors that determine behavior. But I prefer to adopt a different, more inclusive approach. To address effectively the problems we encounter in our daily lives, I believe it's necessary to consider the individual and her social context simultaneously—in other words, to treat a person and her relationships as a single reality.

If what I've just said isn't entirely clear, don't worry. I'll return to the idea later. The point I want to make here is that a parallel exists between the exchanges we routinely engage in in life and movement on the dance floor. When I'm dancing with a partner, my first and foremost goal is to maintain balance, so that no matter what position I'm in or how the dance evolves, I'm poised, composed, and graceful. But it is far more difficult for me to remain poised—to keep from being knocked off-balance—if my partner isn't composed as well. Now, it's true, I could assume a defensive position, bracing for his impact and thus preserving balance. But that isn't dancing, it's combat. The joy of dancing is to move in concert with someone else, to collaborate rather than to confront. Balance, then, is something that's best achieved *together*.

In my view, the same is true of all realms of life. Except in those situations in which we're under attack by people bent on doing harm, a subject that's well beyond the scope of this book, we seek harmonious relationships. I don't mean to imply that there's no room for difference or conflict. Quite the contrary. As is the case in certain dances, tension can heighten drama and raise energy levels, leading to unexpected effects. But underlying the differences is unity of action, a commitment to the partnership, to its well-being and longevity. You may have good reason to get angry, for example, at a spouse or child or coworker, but that doesn't mean you wish to sever the relationship. The challenge is expressing such anger without los-

> ⟨⟨
>
> *(In life)* grace
> *is to* change *as*
> *(in dance)* balance
> *is to* movement.

ing poise or—and this is crucial—destroying the poise of the other person. Speaking more generally, the challenge before us is to remain graceful in the face of any and all changes that may come our way. Dancing, I believe, has much to teach us about that challenge. It gives us a way to talk about it that's easy to grasp. *(In life)* grace *is to* change *as (in dance)* balance *is to* movement. How we deal with the ups and downs, the give and take, of day-to-day existence can be described in terms borrowed from the world of dance. More important, dancing suggests what may be possible when human beings truly do act in concert—creativity, beauty, and, yes, love.

In the chapters that follow I will attempt to show you why the dancing partnership is a model of a constructive relationship, one that applies to every aspect of our lives, from romance to families and friendship to the workplace. I want to warn you, however, that as the discussion unfolds you will notice paradoxes. I'm going to urge you to set goals, for instance, then ask you not to cling to them so intently that you are blinded to new opportunities. My aim isn't to confuse. It's to acknowledge a higher form of balance, to shift, when the situation calls for it, from an "either-or" perspective to a "both-and" one, because in doing so we draw nearer to the heart of existence. *Living is an art, not a science.* When most vibrant, life lies beyond words, sometimes embracing contradiction. Ultimately, it defies description and analysis.

> ⟨⟨
>
> *Living*
> *is an art, not a*
> *science.*

Like dance, living isn't a thought; it's something one does. Like dance, it's in constant flux.

From those of you who are new to dance, have never danced, or, heaven forbid, don't like to dance, I ask patience. The human drama plays out on many stages, and the world of dancing is but one of them. It just so happens that it's the one with which I'm familiar and from which I've drawn the life lessons I've found most useful. I'd wager, however, that a good number of those lessons will ring true among those of you who don't know a two-step from a tango from a step-shuffle-step. So, please dance with me. Take my hand as I take you on a tour of the dance floor. I can't promise it won't be a little awkward, even painful. But who knows? You might have fun. Better yet, you might find yourself doing and accomplishing more than you've ever dreamed of, or as Lerner and Lowe put it "a thousand things [you've] never done before."

TWO

First Steps

I get up. I walk. I fall down.
Meanwhile, I keep dancing.
—HILLEL "THE ELDER"

Have you ever watched a child learning to walk? He grabs hold of a chair leg or the corner of a sofa, pulls himself up, teeters, and tumbles backward. It's inevitable. Or he pushes himself up from the floor, his legs wobbling, then stumbles forward, landing exactly where he started—on his hands and knees. This may happen a hundred, several hundred, a thousand times, maybe more. Who's counting? The child surely isn't. He has only one thing on his mind, and that's putting one foot in front of the other, no matter how many tries it takes. It wouldn't be an exaggeration to say that learning to walk is actually an exercise in falling down, again and again.

And except on those occasions when the child lands on his bottom a little too hard or hits his chin on the carpet, he goes about falling down with obvious glee. He grins and squeals and laughs and plays on. All the more

Persistence is a form of beauty.

noteworthy, the laugh isn't self-conscious. It comes wholly from within the child, a spontaneous expression of the delight he feels in his own movement and accomplishments.

Later, after the falling has ceased, that same child almost certainly will try to dance. Just about everyone does. It's as natural as breathing. If the child's confidence hasn't been weakened or broken by childhood experience, he'll approach dancing the same way he did walking. He'll be fearless and uninhibited. Observing the carefree, improvisational movements of a child, one would have to conclude that dancing is just about the easiest thing in the world to do. But if that's so, why are many of the students who come through the doors of my studio nervous about stepping onto the dance floor? Why are they withdrawn, fearful? Why are their bodies rigid, their muscles tight as a drum? Why are their initial movements stiff, even robotic? And why do they pay so much more attention to how their movements *appear* than to moving itself? Why, in other words, is something that's so easy for the innocent so hard for the experienced? Shouldn't it be the other way around?

*T*he modern Japanese performance art known as Butoh is a highly stylized form of dance practiced by people with extraordinary strength and acrobatic dexterity. Their faces are painted white, their clothing, when they choose to wear it, is spare and uniform in color, and they move extremely slowly and in ways that suggest unseen forces are working upon them, pulling them this way and that, pressing down on them, preventing them from stepping forward. Sometimes the performers seem to be dragging invisible weights behind them, so that everything they do requires great exertion. Every act is met with resistance. Those unseen but inescapable burdens could just as well be what we call baggage. You've heard the term, I'm sure. It applies to situations in which we carry more psychological "stuff" than what's required, and the excess is always something negative, such as an emotional hangover, unresolved grievance, and so on.

Among adults new to dance, baggage is easy to detect. The stiff bodies and rigid movements I spoke of earlier give it away. It's as if they were carrying anvils on their shoulders. Young children, by contrast, haven't had time to accumulate excess emotional weight. They enjoy a certain lightness of being that, regrettably, gets harder to maintain as time goes by. To some extent, of course, the psyche is always expressed physically—in our posture, tone of voice, the relative liveliness of the eyes. But dancing amplifies this reflection. Without knowing what the underlying cause might be—fear, doubt, anger, envy, addiction—it quickly becomes apparent when a student is struggling with invisible burdens or hidden obstacles. Obvious, too, is the similarity to the world beyond the dance floor. Like Butoh dancers, all of us walk through life being pushed, pulled, and stymied by forces that are unseen—and, unfortunately, often ignored.

An important distinction needs to be made, however. I'm speaking here of obstacles over which we have some reasonable hope of exercising control. A person who is severely and chronically abused during childhood may suffer a degree of psychological damage that is, for all practical purposes, impossible to repair. Similarly, some victims of rape and extreme violence never fully recover, not for lack of effort or opportunity but simply and sadly because the act destroyed something elemental in the person's identity—like a bomb hitting the foundation of a house, rendering it permanently unstable or, in extreme cases, shattering it altogether. And we should never lose sight of the countless people in the world who live in terror or impoverishment; are subject to social, political, or religious repression; or whose families, homes, and neighborhoods have been devastated by war. Their plight would be obscenely trivialized and the cause of personal growth made a mockery of were I to propose dancing as a model for redressing such grave conditions. You and I can count ourselves very lucky indeed that we have nothing more weighty to worry about than broken hearts and social anxiety, petty obsessions and thwarted ambitions.

Come to think of it, that's a good place to start—acknowledging that in the grand scheme of things our problems are comparatively minor in both degree and consequence. One way to begin reducing the unwanted effects of your baggage is

> —∅
> *Be gentle*
> *with yourself.*

to place your load, so to speak, in the proper context. Here's another way of saying the same thing: Lighten up and stop taking yourself so seriously. *Be gentle with yourself.* If our aim is to re-capture a little childhood innocence, and I think it should be, then it will help to recognize that we are in fact relatively inno-cent. We haven't been visited by the worst the world has to offer, not even close. In a sense we are still taking our first steps, even though we've got twenty, thirty, forty, or more years of experience under our belts. We therefore have good reason to be lighthearted, willing to risk a fall or two or more to be able to learn something new or achieve something we desire. I'll say it again: Be gentle with yourself.

That some of us nevertheless remain heavy-hearted, I ad-mit, is also a fact of life. Our obstacles may be relatively small, but they still get in the way of living fully and joyfully. How can we take steps toward overcoming them? One of the lessons I've learned from teaching dance is that people start loosening up and growing once they give themselves *permission to begin again.* That's really what our dilemma as adults is: learning to live well and learning to start over, at any-thing or everything, even though we're well into our lives. On the studio dance floor, students are encouraged to begin over and over, as often as they wish. In time, this has the practical effect of re-ducing the fear of failure. If they know they'll have as many opportunities as they

> —∅
> *Give yourself*
> *permission to*
> *begin again—and*
> *again and*
> *again.*

need to get something right, they tend to worry less about getting it right the first time. That makes them more relaxed and more receptive, which in turn lets them concentrate on the routines they are trying to learn and to ignore how they appear for the time being. As they hit their stride, they reach a state that might be called *focused forgetfulness,* when the self recedes into the background altogether and nothing is left but the dance. That's unusual among novices, to be sure, and for that matter not all that common among seasoned professionals, but it gives you a picture of what we strive for—and what you might consider striving for as well.

Where should you begin? Keep in mind that practicing new behavior is much easier if you have a safe environment within which to experiment. The dance floor provides just such a haven for those learning the Western swing or mambo, the ballet steps known as terre-à-terre, or the latest hip-hop moves. Simply walking onto the dance floor can make you feel as if you've left the mundane world behind and entered a charmed realm of expanded possibility. I train my instructors to reinforce the outlook in their students that they are in a place where the old, oppressive social rules don't apply, where mistakes are accorded no great importance, no one is going to ridicule them, nothing they do will diminish the instructor's respect and fondness for them, and the main goal is enjoyment. In short, we try to establish an atmosphere of playfulness, to approximate as nearly as possible the circumstances surrounding our earliest learning experiences, such as mastering the ability to place one foot in front of another. As the first-century

Jewish teacher Hillel observed, "I get up. I walk. I fall down. Meanwhile, I keep dancing."

Likewise, your first steps toward overcoming an internal obstacle are more likely to be successful if you can find or create circumstances in which you feel safe, even encouraged, to experiment. Easier said than done, I know. But everything's easier said than done. So let's retire that complaint for good. It doesn't help us get where we want to go. Among the most obvious protective environments is the therapeutic setting. Leaving aside the sometimes baffling and seemingly contradictory theories counselors, psychologists, and psychiatrists adhere to, the feature all therapeutic settings hold in common is that they give you the latitude to say things you'd be reluctant to utter anywhere else, for fear of hurting, scandalizing, or disappointing others. *I no longer love my husband. I betrayed my best friend. I don't want to have children.* Outside the therapeutic setting, such nakedly candid statements might elicit responses that aggravate rather than alleviate a problem. And it's exceedingly difficult, if not impossible, to overcome an obstacle if you don't have at least some room in your life for speaking openly, without fear of reprisal or recrimination, without having to assume a defensive posture.

Smart people ask for help.

My advice to those who are hopelessly stuck in their lives, the weight so heavy that they risk paralysis and have nowhere else to turn, is to consider seeking professional guidance. In my experience, *successful, healthy people know when and how to ask for help.* This is true even of those who appear to be completely independent, self-made individuals. And if such people didn't explicitly request assistance along the way, you can be sure they received it all the same—from their parents, by virtue of social and financial privilege, or through sheer luck. Nothing could be more wrong-headed than thinking that needing help is a sign of weakness. Actually, just the reverse is true. If you accept the underlying principle of this book—that *you are your relationships as much as anything else*—then turning to others for assistance is an act of self-affirmation. Mull that over for a moment. Your health and well-being depend to a great degree on the health and well-being of everyone with whom you're connected, be it a lover, friend, neighbor, or business partner, and likewise, their health and well-being depends on you. Everyone has a stake in the *relationships,* whether they're aware of it or not. Everyone therefore stands to gain by any one person's attempt to overcome an obstacle to living fully and creatively. It's the equivalent of saying, "I care enough about myself, as well as about the people around me on whom I depend and who depend on me, that I'm going to try to improve the situation." Think of it as an inverted form of the weakest link concept: Anything that strengthens the one, strengthens the many.

Please don't get me wrong. I don't mean to imply that a person can't grow on her own. In later chapters I'll tackle the difficult subject of enabling oneself. But for now we're focusing on getting started, taking the first steps not only toward a more fulfilling life but toward acquiring the perspective and skills necessary to continue growing. We're learning how to learn. And in a culture that continues to perpetuate the myths of rugged individualism and bootstrap ambition despite the accompanying widespread social fragmentation, personal estrangement, and debilitating solitude, it's important at the outset to remind ourselves that we are, in fact, *interdependent*. Were you to ask passersby on a busy city street what troubles them most about their lives, and were they to be honest, chances are high that isolation would appear somewhere on most of their lists. Now, isn't that odd? To feel alone in the midst of a crowd? Surrounded by people with very similar problems yet trying to solve one's own totally alone? I don't know about you, but that seems cockeyed to me. And unnecessary.

That's why I feel strongly that during the first phase of achieving wholeness it's essential we recognize that we are social beings, then look for a social setting in which we feel free to explore new behavior. Ideally, of course, that would occur with those we love most—mate, parent, dear friend. If you and those you're closest to don't already make a habit of confronting obstacles head-on, openly discussing difficult emotional topics, and so on, the best approach is to begin very slowly. Choose a time when there are no distractions, then tell your partner that you're troubled by something and that you'd like his or her help untangling the problem. Should you meet resistance, back off and ask simply that they con-

> *Give as*
> *you want*
> *to get.*

sider what you've said. If the person truly does love you, however, you'll probably receive a sympathetic response. Then explain that to be able to speak freely, you need to know that you're not going to be attacked or punished for what you say.

This sounds more palatable if it's accompanied by expressions of love and support and an offer to return the favor. Give as you want to get.

You'll know the process is working when both of you believe you're confronting a common problem—that you're in it together. I won't kid you. This isn't easy to achieve. Some couples, for example, take years to develop such an outlook. Sadly, others never do. But it's absolutely critical that you avoid accusatory statements that place blame on the other person. *You did this. You didn't do that. You're an awful person. You, you, you.* Any version of these utterances will destroy the spirit of the dance. They will create distance and elicit defensiveness. Instead of moving in concert with your partner you'll find yourself in combat with him, that is, if he hasn't already stormed out of the room. Avoid negative references to character and attend instead to behavior. *You're such a considerate person. It's just not like you to ignore me when we're in public.* And emphasize what *you're* going through—*I don't know, honey, I'm just feeling lonesome lately. Have I done something to disappoint you?*—as opposed to what someone else is doing to you—*Why don't you touch me anymore?*

> *We're in this together.*

To be sure, this is a rudimentary introduction to an extremely difficult and ultimately mysterious area of human experience. Be assured that the ideas presented in simplified form here will be developed over the course of the book and especially in Chapter 8, titled "Duets." Not all of us are going to have the luxury of exploring new behavior in completely or consistently safe environments. We'll have to devote as much energy to creating those environments as to overcoming internal obstacles to growth. This is simply another way of saying that if problems get worked out, they do so within the context of relationships, which requires that you try to increase your awareness of and sensitivity to the obstacles the people you care about are facing. Create a safe environment for them to explore their feelings, to say what normally doesn't get said. Remember the cardinal rule: Ask your partner to cast all statements in terms of "I" instead of "you." *I'm restless. I'm worried. I'm feeling vulnerable.* If your mate, friend, or coworker steadfastly opposes any attempt to address mutual problems, however, it's probably time to reconsider the importance of that particular relationship in your life.

Since many of us will be forced by circumstances to practice new behavior in environments that are only partially or intermittently safe, it helps to know that there are ways we can strengthen our resolve to go forward, taking those first wobbly steps. Apart from active and passive resistance from those around us, the biggest obstacle of all is our own fear of failure. Remember what I said about giving yourself permission to start over again as often as you need to? If you can put this principle into practice you'll go a long way toward transforming your life because the world tends to oblige those who persist and persist and persist. Where, after all, did you learn your concept of failure? And it is *learned,* believe me. Think about it for a moment. Failure wasn't part of your worldview when you were teaching yourself to walk. Nor was fear. You got up,

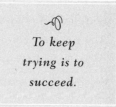

To keep
trying is to
succeed.

you stumbled, you stood again—without giving it a thought. The word *failure* possessed no meaning in that context. And if it did, it would refer to not trying. That's all.

And that's precisely how I urge you to view failure today, tomorrow, and for the rest of your tomorrows. Whatever you may have been taught during your childhood and afterward, *start taking charge of your life by redefining failure as not trying*. Memorize this, meditate upon it, write it in your journal repeatedly, say it aloud before you go to sleep as if it were a prayer. Do everything you can to cultivate the outlook that as long as you are trying, you are succeeding. *Trying is always success.* Expect to trip over yourself. Expect to look foolish at times, to cause misunderstanding, to misstep in any number of ways. But as long as you're stumbling, you're making an effort, and therein lies your success.

> *Life is a contact sport.*

Remember, too, that *life is a contact sport*. Everything that's worth achieving exacts a cost of one kind or another. You can't expect to attempt something as difficult as altering the way you behave without picking up a few bumps and bruises, no more than a baby learning to walk can. Sometimes it's going to hurt. But that's no reason for quitting. If a one-year-old can take the knocks, so can you. Right?

Here's another hint for making it easier to change the way you behave: Start with little steps, and build from there. Give each step a name and *give yourself credit for each step you take, no matter how small*. In other words, define success in as many different ways as possible. For the sake of illustration, let's say that you've done a lot of soul-searching and you've finally

> ⌐◯
> *Give yourself credit for each step you take, no matter how small.*

identified one of your major internal obstacles—an inordinate fear of aggression. Perhaps you had an overbearing parent or sibling or were physically attacked at some point in your life. The cause is far less important than what you intend to do about the consequence. People who are easily intimidated frequently show signs of timidity throughout everything they do, including such mundane activities as getting out of bed and the way they walk in public. My recommendation is that they focus first on everyday activities. If you have a habit of rising from your bed sluggishly, try jumping out of bed. If you're prone to walking with your head down and your shoulders slumped, stand up straight, hold your head up high. Stride. And every time you greet the new day with open arms or make your way down the sidewalk with a bit of a strut, tell yourself, *I'm succeeding.*

This may sound silly, but believe me it works, *but only if you persist, if you try and try again.* Imagine that after years of idleness and overeating you're taking up a new physical activity—lap swimming, for example. You swam in pools and lakes as a kid and occasionally as an adult, so you're more-or-less competent if not terribly proficient or strong. But your goal is to be able to swim one mile without stopping and to do so five days a week. Where do you begin? Relying on a less-than-optimum stroke and being in poor condition, you're certainly not going to complete a mile on your initial attempt. You'll be lucky if you can finish a few laps before becoming exhausted.

Indeed, the first day's effort will fall laughably short of what you hope eventually to achieve. But that's not the point, is it? Rather, the point is that you've started to make a change, and that by consistently building on that change, day in and day out, you actually can bring about a significant difference. It takes time, but it's doable.

*P*sychological change certainly is more complicated, and it invariably is affected by the attitudes, expectations, and behavior of others, but the same principle applies. Starting small holds more promise. And success, even seemingly insignificant success, begets success. Like the lap swimmer's unimpressive initial performance, the timid person's first attempts to take control of her life may seem trivial, but they will embolden her to attempt slightly more ambitious steps, especially if she tells herself and is convinced that small changes are forms of progress. With that to stiffen her backbone, she might next confront someone in a fairly benign setting where the psychological and social consequences are minor—a restaurant, for example. A person who's unduly fearful of aggression may find it hard to express displeasure under any circumstance, even regarding something as minor as the way food is prepared. Being able to send an inadequately cooked meal back to the kitchen could be a crucial link in a series of actions that eventually lead to being able to stand up for oneself in all situations, large or small, from the bedroom to the boardroom.

> *Success begets success.*

26

When I say name your successes, even the smallest of them, I'm speaking literally. Write them down. Research has shown that positive feedback accelerates learning. Remember the times when you tried to lose weight and you stepped on a scale to discover that in fact you had dropped several pounds? You probably felt a surge in confidence, a sense of "I can do this," and that translated into momentum to continue the effort. That's how feedback works. Make it work for you by recording every time you accomplish something new. Ideally, you'll also receive encouragement for positive change from those close to you. That's another way of defining the safe environment I spoke of earlier. I teach my instructors to compliment their students whenever they complete a movement, no matter how slight.

Protect yourself by conserving your energy.

But we shouldn't be blind to the fact that some people take pleasure in discouraging others. The reasons they do so are immaterial. What's important to remember for those taking their initial steps toward behavioral change is that you must keep an eye out for such life-denying people and *protect yourself by conserving your energy,* saving it for more important, more promising work. Imagine the outcome were a parent to punish an infant every time he stumbled. That poor child might never learn to walk. This brings us to one of the most fundamental principles of my teaching system: that everything we do—whether on the dance floor or dancing through life—depends on energy; how much we have, how it flows, how it's wasted or misdirected, and whether others

take away our energy or help replen-
ish it. Always try to choose your
partners—be they spouses, friends,
coworkers, or anyone else—on the
basis of who's most likely to help you
maintain or increase your energy level.
Here's another way to look at it: Take
care of yourself as you would a child
attempting to walk for the first time.
Imagine that you're the parent of that

> ⤴
> *Choose your
> partners on the
> basis of who's most
> likely to help
> you maintain or
> increase your
> energy level.*

child. Were you to ridicule your infant son or daughter every
time he or she stumbled the child would be drained of his or
her natural energy—in other words, her appetite for life. Not
only would she never walk, she would be rendered incapable
of learning anything new.

That's an extreme example, to be sure. But it tells us something memorable about beginning again—that it's never easy,
especially for adults, who tend to believe that their beginnings,
their first steps, are behind them. That's what conventional wisdom would have us think, right? By a certain age, we're supposed to know what we're doing. We're supposed to be in
charge of our lives. But life doesn't actually work this way. It's
not a steady progression from innocence to experience, from
incompetence to mastery, from lack of control to control. Life
is movement. Life is change. Life is renewal. We're continually
presented with new circumstances, new challenges, each of
which calls for a new response—a new beginning. In other
words, to dance through life is to start over again, and again,
and yet again. Make a habit of beginning again, of learning how

> Life is
> movement. Life
> is change.
> Life is renewal.

to begin again. You'll be much better prepared for the twists and turns that lie ahead. You'll be more flexible, resilient, youthful. You won't be paralyzed by obstacles. You won't be immobilized by disappointment or loss. You'll dance through any difficulty or pain you may encounter. You'll *live* through it.

And to help you live through difficulty, develop a supportive environment by surrounding yourself with people who also make a habit of beginning again. In your relationships seek out those who freely offer encouragement, who are willing to risk going through change themselves, who will help you back to your feet when you fall. And you'll fall. Many times. But in the falling you'll learn more about the dance of life than you ever could standing on the sidelines watching others.

THREE

Silencing the Inner Critic

Don't think about it, just do it.
—GEORGE BALANCHINE

Among the many factors of contemporary life
that prevent us from fulfilling our potential,
whether it be within the personal or public realm,
the amount of attention we devote to shortcomings
and failings is especially dismaying. As I mentioned
toward the end of the last chapter, certain sour individuals seem incapable of or unwilling to affirm and
nurture the lives of others, making a habit of un-
dermining confidence, squelching creativity and expression, and, in general, sucking the light out of
every room they enter. But that's not whom I'm talking about here. No, I have in mind decent, ordinary
people whose motivation is usually benign, who try

to do what's right, even if they sometimes fall short or bring about unintended consequences, a result that's next to impossible to avoid in the imperfect world of human affairs. I like to think I'm one of those people. I'm sure you do, too, as do most of those we know. Yet we have a troubling habit of pointing out, making judgments of, and sometimes obsessing over the flaws we see—or think we see—in others, especially those closest to us.

Maybe it's because we live in a highly competitive society that places a heavy emphasis on being the best, the brightest, the wealthiest, the most beautiful—the one and only instead of one of many. Or it simply could be that we haven't figured out a way to help those who depend on us, such as children, mates, and employees, without expressing disapproval. Whatever the reasons may be, I'm convinced that there's a better way—a better way to learn, to grow, and, most important, to live. The process I envision would rely on encouragement rather than discouragement, acceptance rather than judgment, rewarding strength instead of punishing weakness. It would also begin in childhood, indeed, from the day a boy or girl is born. Consider the typical pattern of child rearing today. Parents who are considerate and loving nonetheless slowly erode the fearlessness—*the natural appetite for new experience*—children usually possess in their first years. By what they say and do when their children make mistakes, parents gradually teach the children to be overly cautious, self-conscious, self-condemning, and, worst of all, to associate error with being bad—as if stumbling were a sin. And once that moral equation has been established in someone's mind, it's very hard to erase.

Obviously some behavior requires disapproval in the clearest possible terms. Unprovoked violence, for example, as well as cruelty and selfishness. It's also clear that some parents are more inclined to recklessly employ disapproval and ridicule than others, while some children are more resilient than others, and whatever erosion of confidence may occur is always compounded or tempered to one degree or another by the attitudes of peers, teachers, and everyone else children encounter. Consequently, some of us are relatively unaffected, most of us are hampered to varying degrees, and a few of us are paralyzed. And the damage doesn't end in childhood. We live in a society that promotes individualism while at the same time stigmatizing failure on all levels and in all domains of life, thereby breeding fear—fear of change, fear of attempting something new, fear of being judged harshly by others. Since the aim of this book is to address adult problems in adult contexts, that's all I need say for now about child rearing. The more pressing issue is this: How can we who have fully developed personalities, who have stubborn habits and long-established traits, reduce our fear of failure, thereby weakening and perhaps even undoing the self-destructive equation that says that if you stumble when you're learning to walk you're morally wrong as well.

It's our natural state to be motivated and to want new experience.

When I said earlier that you must protect yourself from those who constantly and carelessly disapprove of what you say and do, I was referring to anyone in your life, but especially those you love and those who profess to love you, because you are by definition most vulnerable to them and therefore easily harmed. But there's another unrelenting and frequently more severe judge who's by your side day and night—the voice in your head, which I call the *inner critic*. You may have more than one. In fact, an entire chorus may provide nonstop stinging commentary as you go about your life. You know what I mean. Every one of us struggles with internal critics whose only job, it seems, is to convince us that we're losers and that there's nothing we can do about it. I see the phenomenon all the time on the dance floor in the nervousness and distraction of new students. They're only partially present, their attention drawn elsewhere, toward the dialogue that's taking place within. Too busy following that internal argument, they can't fully concentrate on the world immediately before them, which makes learning unnecessarily difficult.

One of casualties of the inner critic, then, is awareness. Whenever we pay heed to the critic *we waste energy* we could otherwise use for the task at hand. Understanding the relationship between energy and attention is essential to personal development. Specifically, where you direct your energy—what you attend to from one moment to the next—will either help you grow and make you stronger or keep you stagnant and make you weaker. Some people are so numb from fear, self-doubt, or self-loathing that they scarcely notice anything going on around them, still fewer respond in suitable ways. They sleepwalk through life, doing only what's minimally necessary to function. Most of us aren't this bad off, but nonetheless we aren't fully present all of the time. We converse without being entirely aware of what we're saying. We listen to others without paying full attention to what they're saying. We watch the world without really looking closely at what's taking place. A sure sign that this is happening is forgetfulness. If you find that you can't recall recent events or encounters, in all likelihood it's because you weren't really *present* when they occurred. Another sign, the one that concerns us most here, is an inability to acquire new knowledge or skills.

Have you ever heard the comment, "There is no *there* there"? The very witty writer Gertrude Stein famously said that about Oakland, California, where she once searched in vain for her childhood home. The phrase sometimes comes to mind when I look into people's eyes and see that they have directed their energy inward, away from living, per se, to their worrisome thoughts about living. There's no there there, no one looking back at me. And it's spooky. When I was a dance instructor I sometimes felt as if I were competing for my students' attention, trying to turn their focus toward me, toward the movements I was trying to teach on the dance floor and away from whatever debilitating nonsense was playing over and over again in their minds. That's another feature of the inner critic: repetition. The critic never has anything new to say. Many good impulses and worthwhile ideas enter our minds unbidden. The way to distinguish such welcome inspiration from the critic is that the latter offers the same message of discouragement day in and day out. It's always the same: *You can't do it. You're a fool for trying. It would be best if you just went home and crawled into bed.*

> *The inner critic wastes energy you need for growth.*

Withdrawal from the world. Watching from the sidelines of life rather than plunging in and participating. That's the critic's ultimate aim. And that's just another way of saying that the critic is in league with death. Maybe that statement seems exaggerated to you. But after observing the destruction inner critics have caused in countless people in my personal and professional life, I'm convinced that we are dealing with the forces of darkness—all that would pull us away from the sun and its life-giving light toward the grave. I've seen people in whom the internal dialogue is so loud and insistent that it actually overrides external information that conveys exactly the opposite. Chances are you've witnessed this dynamic as well. In mild cases, it shows up as a person's inability to accept a compliment. At the extreme end of the spectrum are those lonely souls whose internal criticism so undermines their sense of self-worth that they are rendered incapable of receiving love. They can't bring themselves to believe that they'll ever be worthy of deep affection and thus view any such expression as fraudulent or misguided or simply a source of confusion. Consequently, they avoid all forms of intimacy.

> *The inner critic wants you to turn your back on life.*

What I've just described is called a self-fulfilling prophecy. Convinced that she's of no value to anyone, the person who's enslaved to her critic behaves in ways that confirm the negative presumption, distancing herself from any situation in which the internal voice might be contradicted. No matter how desperate for companionship she may become, she'll

take steps to ensure her own isolation. Often she'll be un-
aware of what she's doing. There's a memorable lesson to be
learned here and it's this: Though the inner critic may appear
to be acting on your behalf, trying to spare you humiliation
and the agony of failure, it doesn't have your best interests in
mind, not in the least. Remember what I said earlier: It's natural for healthy human beings to be
motivated, to hunger for new experience, to want to grow. Children
come into the world fearless, eager
to experiment, giving no concern to
whether they stumble along the way.

*You can
never please the
inner critic.*

Fear of disapproval is something we learn from the voices in
our social environment. We also have the tendency to *inter-
nalize* the voices we are exposed to, especially those we hear
during our formative years. The original environment almost
always will be long gone, yet the voices remain as strong as
ever.

Now that you know you face a severe test, I want to assure
you that the inner critic can be challenged and subdued. Rarely
is it silenced altogether, I admit, but its power can be reduced to
a level that any damage or disruption it may cause will be min-
imal or at least short-lived. The battle begins—and, trust me, it's
a battle—by recognizing the enemy and its potential for doing
you harm. The inner critic traffics in nothing but fear and doubt
and it does so ad nauseam. It also masquerades as your friend,
pretending to protect you from pain when it actually is depriving
you of pleasure. *If you're not willing to risk falling, you'll never
learn to walk.* That principle applies to every new experience in

> *If you're not willing to risk falling, you won't learn to walk.*

your life. A third characteristic of the critic is that *it cannot be pleased*. The voice that stands in judgment of your every word and deed will never be satisfied. From its standpoint, you'll always be a failure. It's very existence depends on your failing. That fact alone reveals that we are dealing with an insidious, self-destructive part of the personality. And the closer we get to life, to the wellsprings of growth and creativity and expression, the more displeased it becomes.

As with any attempt to alter the course of behavior, begin gradually. Start by observing when the inner critic emerges and how it operates. Pay particular attention to the circumstances in which the voice becomes intense and insistent, and especially when it actually stops you from acting on an urge that is healthy in every other respect. Maybe your critic grows loud and disruptive whenever you meet an attractive woman whom you'd like to ask out on a date, or when a superior at work expects you you to come up with new ideas. Maybe you long to tell your husband that you've grown tired of your usual social routines and wish to try something different, but the voice always cuts you off at the last moment, causing you to hold your tongue. Or perhaps you've always wanted to speak Spanish, or travel abroad, or learn how to do the hula, but your inner critic has convinced you that you're dumb and clumsy and the effort would end in disaster, so don't even bother. Do you see the common thread? In every one of these instances a desire is thwarted. Desire—all that motivates us, animates us, makes us glad to get up in the morning—is the manifestation of the life force, the energy that drives the entire biological world. In your effort to put the critic in his place, you are siding with life, not only your own but *all* of life. Instead of blocking or diverting the energy of life, you are allowing it to flow through you.

Tell yourself this: *When I ignore the critic, I affirm life.* And do it repeatedly. But to be able to ignore the internal voice of disapproval and discouragement, you must be prepared to withstand a certain amount of inconsistency. It's a psychological fact that the self seeks coherency, or a measure of agreement between feeling and action. To be at odds with oneself is troubling. In the most extreme instances, it's maddening. Literally. You

> *When you ignore the inner critic, you affirm life.*

sometimes see this in people who were physically abused by parents who at the same time expressed undying love for their children. The personality collapses under the weight of the contradiction between the pain the child experienced and the message the parent delivered. Suffering and affection are hopelessly intertwined. This is an extreme example. What you have to contend with is far less serious, but it'll require vigilance and perseverance all the same. You may want to consider adopting a rebellious attitude, because once you're sure that the inner critic prevents you from living a full life, you're going to have to engage in what amounts to acts of defiance. You're going to have to endure a little tension—between the habitual way you've thought of yourself (the impoverished view promoted by the inner critic) and what you truly can become. If you're lucky enough to derive a little pleasure from that, your work will be made easier. Don't pass it up. Be bold. Defy the critic within.

Just as you should protect yourself from those who tend to disapprove of anything new, so should you seek the company of those who'll contradict your inner critic. It's amazing and sometimes frightening to see how domineering an internal voice can be, but having alternative voices in your immediate environment who refuse to go along with the inner criticism can give you the courage to ignore the critic, at least for short periods of time. You want a team in your corner, so to speak, that appreciates the nature and severity of your inner critic— this means you have to be honest with them about your fears and doubts—and that will always cheer you on and back you up, no matter how often you fall. The ideal team refuses to let you be defeated by your own weaknesses. Based on what I've said so far about mates, friends, coworkers, and so on, you may be getting the impression that I believe it's easy to leave people who hinder our growth and find others who enhance it. I certainly don't believe that. Indeed, nothing could be harder. But I do firmly believe that if you're committed to overcoming the obstacles that have prevented growth and squandered your potential, you must give serious consideration to the condition of your relationships. How healthy are they? Personal change is difficult enough. Change in the face

> *Surround yourself with people who won't let you be defeated by your own weaknesses.*

of relentless disapproval or derision or indifference from those who are closest to us is almost impossible.

Some resistance is to be expected, of course. Change makes everyone nervous. And you surely want to give those you love, as well as those who depend on you emotionally or materially, the opportunity to join you in your attempt to live with grace and generosity in an uncertain world. But don't be naïve. Recognize the hard truth that some relationships will drain all the energy you have and still remain unchanged. These may be relationships you think you can't live without. And perhaps that's true. In my opinion, however, *the inability to live without those who habitually hurt us is one of the fundamental problems of human existence*, and it's largely responsible for the development and maintenance of the inner critic, among other undesirable effects. Sometimes the situation is involuntary (as in the case of a child dependent on cruel or psychologically manipulative parents), other times voluntary (as in the case of the adult who plays the role of needy child in his intimate relationships), but it's always destructive. Look at it this way: We participate in the dance of life only briefly. As many others have pointed out, this miraculous opportunity isn't a rehearsal. This is your one and only chance to take advantage of what life has to offer. How do you want to spend your time? Here's another way to put it: How much do you respect yourself? *People with a high level of self-respect know when to walk away from the destructive behavior of others.*

> *People with a high level of self-respect know when to walk away from the destructive behavior of others.*

Few relationships are black-and-white propositions, to be sure. Most commonly, those we care about both help us and hurt us—hurt us accidentally, of course, but with real, occasionally long-lasting results. And we do the same to them. Life being a contact sport, *it's difficult to get close to others without everyone getting bruised.* In short, there are no formulas, no pat answers, no fail-safe approaches that work in all situations. Every principle that I articulate in this book is subject to qualification, depending on circumstances. In this instance I'm obliged to offer the following qualification: Although you can never please an inner critic, it could be helpful to identify the person behind the voice, so as to better understand what's at stake and why. Often the voice is, in fact, a compilation of several voices—all the authority figures you've encountered in your life—and no one individual is implicated. But from the crowd of naysayers and accusers sometimes a clearly defined figure emerges. A parent, for instance.

> *It's difficult to get close to others without everyone getting bruised.*

By clearly defined, I don't mean that the figure is an exact replica of a real parent. The images we carry of those who've made the greatest impressions upon us are combinations of perception, desire, memory, and several other psychological elements. That said, it's also true that certain parents mistreat their children to varying degrees, from unwarranted scolding to physical abuse. Anyone who's been subjected to such behavior over a long period of time is likely to find that her chief inner critic bears a strong resemblance to the original. More often than not, however, the original is no longer available. The parent has died or is unwilling or incapable of discussing the relationship, still less trying to repair it. But even in those cases, it can prove useful to put a name to the internal voice. Naming things is one way to begin gaining power over them. Knowing that you constantly attack and subvert yourself because you have internalized someone else's voice takes you one step closer to reducing the impact of that voice. It's entirely possible that you may have to put up with your mother's disapproval or your father's disappointment for the rest of your life, such is the strength of internalization. But you don't have to *care* as much as you do today or let it cripple you. You may be unable to resolve a problem from the past or reach reconciliation with your actual parent, but you can do so with the parent within. You can reduce the critic's power over you.

Having detected a parent (or any other particular figure from life) behind your internal voice, try imagining that person's internal voice, or voices. In all likelihood, he or she was tormented as well. And at least part of the solution was to project the resulting feelings of inadequacy and failure onto those closest and most vulnerable, including you. This may be regrettable, but it's all too common. So in effect, when you try to please the inner critic you are reacting not only or solely to that parent but to all those unappeasable and unapproachable figures who came before—a jury of distant ancestors whose only verdict is guilty. Don't you find this absurd? Sure, all of us want to be the apple of our parents' eyes. And those of us who have received the

Everyone needs approval.

unconditional love that families aspire to but frequently fail to provide are extremely fortunate. But those who have not aren't necessarily doomed to lives of misery and solitude. Yes, we need approval. Everyone does. We simply must find new ways to meet that need.

It may appear contradictory, on the one hand, to advise that you free yourself from the tyranny of your inner critic while, on the other, insist that everyone needs approval. What I mean is this: We need to know that we and what we do are valued. This is fundamental to being human. It's much-needed nourishment for the will and inspiration for the soul. Being worthy in the eyes of others is as important to psychological well-being as food is to physical well-being. This need for affirmation is another sign of the preeminence of relationships. Anyone who tells you differently misunderstands the fundamentally social nature of human identity. Where we cause ourselves unnecessary difficulty is when we seek affirmation from the wrong people or for the wrong reasons. The inner critic is a manifestation of looking to the wrong individual for approval, because it never approves of anything except giving up and giving in. Only when you succumb to your weaknesses or abandon your effort to overcome an obstacle will the critic change its tone: *That's right, you're a failure. You always have been. You always will be. And don't ever forget it.* No longer is there any tension between what the critical interior voice says and how you behave. And with that a certain calmness may set in—the peace of the defeated.

> *Find new, healthier ways to meet your need for approval.*

Make no mistake, personal growth almost always causes discomfort. To live more fully, you'll have to resist the tendency to make peace with your weaknesses. Given a choice between the comfort of defeat and the discomfort of the struggle, many people will choose the former, even if it involves severe psychological deprivation. Such deprivation and the needless personal drama surrounding it can become addictive. The situation resembles that of the person who deliberately cripples himself or his child so that they have a means—begging—for surviving a life of impoverishment. However, you wouldn't go to, impose, or accept such an extreme if you weren't somehow convinced that you deserve impoverishment and that anything more than that exceeds your rightful station. I know individuals who starve for love, who are emotionally poverty stricken, yet they subvert every situation in which real, enduring affection might arise. They've become addicted to their

> Personal growth
> always causes
> discomfort.

image of themselves as lonely, unwanted persons, victims of circumstances beyond their control, and from that misguided standpoint it makes perfect sense to subsist on the emotional scraps that others, acting out of pity, toss their way. Theirs, however, is a diet of bitterness, one that over time yields anemic, emaciated psyches, sometimes generations of them.

I'm assuming that since you're reading this book you aren't one of these people, or at least you recognize the early warning signs of the syndrome I just outlined. Mild forms of self-induced psychological impoverishment are in fact quite common. Every time we lick our wounds, taking pleasure in the pain that's been inflicted upon us, we risk turning weakness into a badge of honor. We cultivate excuses for choosing acquiescence over courage. Remember what I said earlier about contradictions between thought and feeling, perception and action? The tension that results is so disturbing that we'll go to great lengths to relieve it, even if it requires doing damage to ourselves. This is because what's at stake is nothing less than our identity, our sense of self. Identity is how we convert the chaos of experience into something recognizable, familiar, and comforting. It's how we give meaning to the countless random events of our day-to-day existence. It's how we tie one moment to the next, so that we experience our lives as a continuous process rather than a series of disconnected fragments. One of the key ingredients of identity is consistency, in particular, between our sense of self and how we think and act. Maintaining consistency in the midst of constant change is a largely unconscious dynamic that's far too complicated to describe here. What's important to remember is that consistency can be achieved in both negative and positive ways, which explains why for some people it makes perfect sense to avoid opportunities for personal development, even to the extent of crippling themselves.

Allow me to explain. When our picture of our self is at odds with how we behave, it's virtually impossible to feel at home in the world. We become *estranged* from our environment. At the same time we start to experience a parallel estrangement within, as if our psyche were splitting in two. Now imagine that that picture of the self is dominated by the inner critic. One way to bring the picture back into alignment with behavior, restoring unity within and peace without, is to accept the harsh judgment of the inner critic without question. Though this approach holds an appeal that's fairly obvious, it certainly is a false bargain. It seems you are resolving a problem, but instead you're putting your life on hold, preventing any possible further growth, a state that can't be sustained without doing damage to yourself. But there's a second way to achieve consistency, by rendering the disapproving voice less important and thereby reducing its influence over your behavior. You'll be glad to hear that a number of techniques and strategies exist for doing exactly this. Indeed, this book as a whole can be viewed as a how-to manual for diminishing the power of the inner critic, for overcoming fear and doubt and getting out on the dance floor of life.

In addition to naming the critic, identifying the pivotal figures responsible for instilling the inner voice, avoiding those who incessantly echo the critic's disapproval and discouragement, and surrounding yourself with people who oppose the critic's judgments and always urge you to do likewise, you can begin to take control of your internal dialogue by introducing a new voice, one that you create as a counterpoint to the critic. I recommend that you write down your positive statements and say them aloud to yourself. And in so doing, I want to add, I'm not promoting the view that merely thinking something makes it so. If that were the case—imagine for a moment the weird, even scary welter of urges, images, and ideas that go through your mind and the minds of those around you—the world would be a chaotic, highly hazardous place indeed. But we should recognize the power of thought. What, after all, is

> ⟋
> *Make a
> habit of thinking
> positively.*

the inner critic but thought? Thought so reinforced through habit that it sometimes seems like part of one's anatomy. Counter the destructive influence of the inner critic by doing the opposite: *Make a habit of thinking positively.* If you tell yourself often enough that you can do something, that you will do it, in time you'll find your self-perception changing. You'll gradually come to see yourself as someone who acts instead of retreats, who takes steps forward, who faces the world rather than turns his back on it. You'll begin to appreciate the value of self-approval, the pride and satisfaction that come from making a courageous effort.

Which is no guarantee, need I remind you again, against stumbling and falling. You will not sidestep rejection, disappointment, and loss. Yes, cultivate a positive attitude, but don't be a fool, don't close your eyes to the way the world actually works. Keep in mind that you're part of a continually shifting, complex web of relationships that greatly exceeds human comprehension and over which we exercise precious little control. From time to time, I'll return to the perennial human problem of the gap between what we want and what we get, but what's important to bear in mind now is that in addition to equipping yourself with an orientation that gives you a fighting chance against the inner critic, adopting a positive *yet clear-eyed* point of view better prepares you for dealing with disappointment and loss. That's because thinking positively includes telling

> ⟋
> *Don't think
> about it, just
> do it.*

yourself that falling down is to be expected and represents no great setback, no more than it does to the child learning to walk. Every time you're faced with a choice, *picture yourself as an active agent in the world who considers persistence to be a form of achievement* instead of a passive victim who looks upon every misstep as a confirmation of the inner critic's accusations. If you do, you'll increase your resiliency, your ability to recover when you do encounter obstacles to growth.

Also keep in mind that our own action also speaks to us. In fact, it's louder than words, if the familiar adage can be believed. Name many ways to achieve success—every little step that goes into bringing about a specific change—and recite them back to yourself with every step you take. In this way you can turn your own behavior into positive feedback that proves the falsity of internal criticism: *See, you did it. You actually did it. And there, you did it again.* Sure, this takes some daring, along with a measure of psychological flexibility. Fear and doubt, the twin engines of internal criticism, lead to rigid thinking, and rigid thinking makes people desperate. And it's all but impossible to see clearly or to act creatively when you're desperate. You may

> *Rigid thinking makes people desperate.*

then feel trapped or without recourse. So, slow down. Tell yourself that you are more than meets the eye or the mind, that you are capable of things no one dreamed you'd ever do. Then, plunge in. That's right. Don't look, don't hesitate. One, two, three, jump! As the brilliant choreographer George Balanchine advised his ballet dancers, *"Don't think about, just do it."*

To be sure, Balanchine's dancers were people with years of

training who under his guidance had rehearsed certain specific routines again and again. But we can learn much from that example. Even at their level of skill and accomplishment, such performers develop a mature performance only through the painstaking process of adding one small step to another, of starting and stopping and starting again, of continuing despite the missteps, miscues, and mishaps. Gradually, their movement becomes easier. They then don't have to try so hard. Even better, they give up trying, abandon thinking, and simply become one with the dance. In a word, it takes time, lots of it, which from the standpoint of the dancer translates as commitment. That's what lasting behavioral change, the kind that leads to personal growth, asks of you. *Commitment.* Are you willing to take the time to learn how to walk again and in a number of different social settings? Will you ignore the criticism of the inner critic and allow yourself to believe that you're going to be successful? Trust me, you have nothing to lose by doing so, and more to gain than you ever imagined.

FOUR

Dance of Desire

*Now I know that you must draw
people to you, like a magnet—perhaps by
the intensity of your own belief.*

—MARTHA GRAHAM

Something I said in the last chapter bears mentioning again: Everyone needs a certain amount of approval, and on a fairly regular basis. Approval is a necessary form of psychological nourishment, without which we would shrivel up and withdraw from the world. But that need also makes us vulnerable, especially to those we love, admire, or depend upon for our well-being, in other words, our primary relationships.

Leaving aside for now the subject of reducing the harmful effects of those relationships, I want to turn to a more immediate problem, one that I frequently encounter during the training programs I conduct for dance studio staff and managers—lack of motivation. After being told repeatedly what they're not capable of doing, what they shouldn't ever attempt to do, or after being punished for making the attempt, some people forget what they really desire. They've been bombarded by so much disapproval and discouragement that they lose sight of what might actually bring them happiness. When I ask those in this unfortunate state to set goals for themselves, they draw a blank, or become paralyzed by the contradictory impulses vying for attention inside them. "I don't know what I want," they say meekly and a little bewildered, resembling an amnesiac who puzzles over his inability to recall his name or occupation or where he lives.

I use the word *amnesiac* deliberately. Memory is essential to who we are. Without it identity vanishes. Think of the most extreme case—those with Alzheimer's disease. During the course of that degenerative condition, one layer of life experience after another is erased, in an almost perfect yet insidious reversal of the normal process of human development. At first the person is merely absent-minded or easily distracted. Then he loses the ability to perform everyday tasks, such as putting on clothes and preparing a meal, and eventually fails to recognize friends, family, even his spouse. As the illness progresses, he becomes incapable of such elementary skills as controlling his bladder and bowels. And with each loss the personality shrinks, until little or nothing of the original, mature, multidimensional individual remains.

Desire can be thought of in similar terms. At times, certainly, desire is destructive, particularly when it takes the shape of insatiable ambition, a disproportionate urge to dominate or possess, or the many kinds of obsession and addiction that humans find themselves enslaved to and consumed by (I'll say more about these later). But what I have in mind here is something simpler, more fundamental. Desire, as I'm employing the term, means that which energizes us to engage with the world around us. It's that mysterious force that draws us forward and outward, toward other people, new experiences, opportunities to learn and grow and taste more of what life has to offer. Anyone who's felt it, and everyone has at one time or another, knows what I mean. How can I be so confident as to say that? All I need do is think of children again. Ask a healthy child what he or she wants and in all likelihood you'll elicit a stream of responses. That's because children haven't yet been trained to suppress their wants or to subordinate them to the wants of others. They haven't been persuaded—I'd go even further to say conned into believing—that it's hopeless, even morally wrong, to request and seek what they really wish for.

> *Desire is the energy that moves us forward and outward— toward life and the living.*

I put this observation into practice whenever I encounter someone in my training workshops who says he can't think of any goals he'd like to pursue. I ask him to turn his attention from the here-and-now to his boyhood. As a child, I explain, everyone had dreams. "What did you want back then?" I ask. Or, stated differently, "What did you want to be when you grew up?" If as you read this, you're also finding it difficult to envision what exactly you want, I suggest you try the same exercise. Even if your desires are apparent, you'll likely benefit by it.

Carefully review your early years. Try to recall moments when you were enthused about some person, activity, event, place, idea, and so on—anything, really, that made your heart beat a little faster. Reinvoke instances of excitement, anticipation, joy, deep satisfaction. Maybe what comes to mind isn't an episode from early childhood but your teenage years or even later in life. In any case, attach names to those moments and instances when you truly wanted something, or got what you wanted, or realized that what accidentally came your way was something you wanted more of. It may happen that the very things you've forgotten you wanted or long-ignored are in fact still highly desirable. Or your exploration of old desires may serve as a catalyst for recognizing what promises to excite you today. Either way, you're now in a better position to articulate your elemental likes and dislikes, which is the first step toward identifying worthwhile goals.

I understand that connection, you may say, but why is setting goals important? First and foremost, they provide direction. As the old saying goes, "If you don't know where you're going, every road will get you there." In other words, being directionless is indistinguishable from being lost. That may seem obvious to you, especially stated that way. But it's precisely what's most obvious and sensible that frequently proves the most difficult to put into practice. Clearly, certain unusual individuals lead fascinating, fulfilling lives without developing a blueprint beforehand. Many artists, for instance, have the ability to reinvent themselves as they go, much as a jazz musician improvises. Indeed, people of this temperament take great pleasure in not planning ahead, believing instead that chance and uncertainty are necessary to the creative process. But few of us are as imaginative, self-driven, or dependent upon the unexpected as artists. Don't get me wrong. Everyone needs a measure of spontaneity and surprise because that keeps life fresh and stimulating. But the challenge we face is both more common and at times more challenging than that of the artist who thrives on spontaneity: selecting from all of life's possibilities what's truly most important to us, then arranging our day-to-day existence accordingly. Only then can we develop a successful defense against the distractions that would prevent us from full enjoyment of the particular pleasures life has in store for each of us. Only then can we establish the consistent focus that's needed to bring our deepest desires to fruition, an endeavor that takes time, usually a great deal of it.

Goals provide direction.

This brings us to an important distinction: the difference between short-term and long-term goals. To live well—which is to say fully engaged yet graceful and generous—we need both. Equally important, we need to appreciate the relationship between the two, so that we're better prepared to make them work in harmony. The most effective short-term goals are specific. They also are highly doable. That probably seems readily apparent and easy enough to accomplish. But for those who have little practice with establishing a clearly marked course for themselves,

Short-term goals are specific and highly doable.

setting and meeting short-term goals can be a good deal harder than one might think. Recall that in Chapter 2 I talked about the power of identifying and naming small successes. This is another way of saying the same thing, except now I'm stressing that being specific is the secret to success.

Let's say, for instance, that you're overwhelmed. Your life is a storm of demands, expectations, responsibilities, or possibilities, causing you to become disoriented or discouraged. What should you do? You won't achieve much if you take "not being overwhelmed" as your goal. Such a generalized objective provides no guidance whatsoever regarding what to do today, at this hour, in this specific place. How would you know where to start? And lacking that, how would you know if you succeeded at what you set out to do? It would be far better for you to select a minor demand (expectation, responsibility, or possibility) and try to satisfy it. And I mean minor. Let's say that you have long-overdue library books or a friend's clothing that she wants back. Write down the task and then do it. Add similarly modest aims to your list—altering what you eat for breakfast, cleaning the car, answering that upsetting e-mail your sister sent two weeks ago—and systematically complete each one. In all likelihood, at the end of the day you'll feel at least slightly more in control of your existence and a little clearer about what to do next.

Now I'm going to introduce one of the paradoxes I talked about earlier. Again, I must stress that I do so not to complicate matters unnecessarily but rather to try to remain faithful to the complexity and changeability of lived experience. What I'm about to say may be easier to grasp, however, if I first provide some background. Bear with me for a moment as I walk you through intellectual terrain that may be unfamiliar. Don't be intimidated. This won't be hard, and it'll give you a powerful new way to look at the world. Have you heard of America's only homegrown school of philosophy? It's called pragmatism,

Ideas are tools.

and it's based on the seemingly simple but surprisingly fruitful assumption that ideas should be treated as tools. According to this perspective, a notion or belief is valuable only to the extent that it's *useful*. Pragmatists are less concerned about the truth of an idea than whether it helps one get things done. A good idea is one that works.

This may strike you as odd or, if you hold strong moral or religious views, even offensive. Like virtually everyone, you probably consider certain principles to be the equivalent of bedrock—the unshakable foundation that gives you a sure footing in life. And I certainly wouldn't ask that you think differently. But for the sake of self-growth and especially the developmental process I promote, I suggest that you adopt a pragmatist approach to the ideas discussed in this book, for example, the idea of setting short-term goals. Yes, as I said, being specific when identifying day-to-day objectives is valuable, but—and this is where the paradox arises—it's also possible to be too specific. That leads to at least two kinds of needless difficulty. On the one hand, you can become so fixated on certain small outcomes that you blind yourself to more promising opportunities for pleasure or accomplishment. Cleaning the basement may be a good use of a Saturday afternoon on some occasions but not when a man you're attracted to asks you out on a picnic. On the other hand, your attachment to short-term outcomes can grow so strong that not being able to attain them brings on a sense of disappointment all out of proportion to circumstances. Failing to lose weight during the first week of a twenty-four-week fitness program, for instance, isn't sufficient cause to sink into a depression.

Remember: Ideas are tools. And like tools, some ideas are better suited to certain tasks than others. One way to define wisdom, then, is the ability to weigh the advantages and disadvantages of the tools at your disposal and to select one that's right for the job. In the case of personal growth, what you'll discover is that usually some combination of tools is required. (Think of this book as a personal growth toolbox.) Setting short-term goals is a tool. So is setting long-term goals. But the power to bring about change lies in using them together. In fact, the two should always be employed in tandem. Being guided by short-term goals can restore a sense of purpose

> *Select the right tools for the job.*

and accomplishment on a day-to-day basis. On the other hand, being guided by long-term goals allows you to see daily setbacks or seemingly insignificant steps as part of a longer, more ambitious process. But it's only when short-term thinking serves long-term thinking that you achieve direction, establishing a course that will steer you successfully through life's perils and pleasures.

Maybe what I've just said seems a little abstract. So let's

consider an example. How about the woman I mentioned earlier—call her Sally—who must choose between cleaning her basement on a Saturday afternoon or going on a romantic outing with a man who interests her? Hardly a choice at all, right? The basement can wait. But what if Sally's basic problem isn't forming relationships but instead lack of control and concentration, disorganization, an inability to complete projects? What if this problem has gone on so long and is so crippling that she's never been able to advance in her job and consequently sees herself as an utter failure and without value to anyone? If her long-term goal is to restore order to her life and thereby gain some much-needed confidence, then foregoing the picnic probably makes sense. Staying home, while disappointing in the short run, would serve her larger purpose. If, on the other hand, Sally's basic problem is fear of new experiences, especially with men, choosing the basement, while worthy in itself, would represent a retreat from life. In the absence of long-term goals, in other words, it's impossible to know whether this or that short-term goal is appropriate.

Short-term goals should serve long-term goals.

The world, to be sure, is both more complicated and less predictable than this example suggests. For one thing, Sally's situation begs the question of what exactly those long-term goals should be. And that takes us back to the discussion that opened this chapter—regarding desire in the best sense of the word. I believe firmly that at the most fundamental level, human needs are fairly simple. Everyone needs a sense of accomplishment, value to others, belongingness, and efficacy (the ability to be effective, to influence the world we live in). And everyone needs a certain amount of love, preferably the unconditional kind. How we go about fulfilling these needs varies wildly, of course, and that's one of the bases for individual difference, which means that it's up to the individual to decide what the best approach may be. Only you can know whether, for instance, your need for belongingness should be met through family relationships, work affiliations, neighborhood and community activities, recreational pursuits, or any other outlets. In all likelihood, more than one and perhaps all of these will be involved to one degree or another.

The fact that fundamental needs potentially can be fulfilled in a number of contexts and under different conditions points to another complexity that shouldn't be overlooked or played down: goals in conflict. Single-mindedness is rare, and when it does exist it's sometimes a symptom of psychological imbalance. Most of us are made up of competing desires and contradictory ambitions. In reality, Sally probably has good reason both to go to work on her cluttered basement *and* accept the invitation to play with a new friend. So what's she supposed to do? Well, one option that's not open to her is to do both, not at the same time, at any rate. I'm stating the obvious to underscore an important feature not only of how individuals evolve but of the overall human condition. Conviction is required if you're going to live to the fullest, which means that choice is unavoidable. A decision will have to made. *This* will be sacrificed for *that*.

> *Conviction is needed for a full life.*

That may sound like bitter medicine. Yet it's actually the key to accomplishment in all areas of our lives. You'll never experience the deep satisfaction of a long romantic partnership unless you make a commitment to a single individual. You'll never excel at an occupation unless you devote yourself to it to the exclusion of other possible lines of work. You'll never realize the potential of your garden unless you tend to it day in and day out, through all kinds of weather, even though you do so at the cost of forgoing other desirable activities. There are no guarantees, of course. But neither is there much hope of enjoying life's greatest pleasures if you don't take a stand, if you don't adopt a point of view.

Should making a choice between conflicting goals seem impossible, should you find yourself paralyzed by the alternatives before you, keep in mind the pragmatic outlook—that a good idea is an idea that works. Then consider the inverse of that statement: An idea that works is a good idea. Take another moment to ponder the implications of that. A workable idea is a worthy idea. How do you know it's workable? Only by acting on it. In short, try an idea on for size and see what happens.

Choose something that's consistent with the person you most want to be—that will reinforce a certain desirable identity. Then give yourself permission to experiment, always defining the attempt itself as success, and allow experience to tell you what you need to know. Discover what really does fulfill you—not through guessing or wondering but through doing, by taking action. Life, as I said early on, is beyond words, beyond

> *Ideas that work are good ideas.*

thought. And if you make the wrong choice, then pause to acknowledge it, correct your course, and head in another direction. It won't be easy. But there's no other way to grow, nor to reawaken desire should it have been squelched.

I should point out that the exercise I've just described will force you to address any problems regarding self-image that you may have, as well as may have been trying to avoid. When developing short-term goals that agree with your preferred identity you could discover that your self-image is unhealthy, embarrassing, or otherwise less flattering than what you would hope. In this instance, which is quite common, the right goals can't be specified or properly adjusted until the inadequate self-image is corrected, because self-images tend to be self-reinforcing. In other words, a negative self-image, breeds destructive behavior. Replacing that image with one that's positive won't happen overnight. Indeed, cultivating a healthy, expansive sense of self is an ongoing enterprise, one that lasts your entire lifetime. But you can become more actively and conscientiously engaged in the process, and you can do so immediately, starting where you are at this very moment. The first step is answering the following questions as honestly as possible: How would you prefer to describe yourself? How does that more positive picture differ from the way you actually see yourself?

Once you have a clear view of the discrepancies between the two images, try to identify any bad habits that are congruent with the less desirable ones. Maybe you see yourself as someone who's financially irresponsible. What do you do that's consistent with that image, that fulfills the negative prophecy you've made about yourself? Do you splurge or spend impulsively when you're short of funds? Do you postpone balancing your checkbook until it's too late? Do you run up debts without thinking through how you'll pay them off? These are precisely the bad habits you must change, and the most effective way to do so is to simultaneously adopt a new self-image and new behavior. Tell yourself that you're fully capable of being financially responsible, then designate one small change that will be consistent with that image. When you've success-

> *Create a new, self-fulfilling prophecy by cultivating a more positive self-image.*

fully completed that change, repeat the procedure. Picture yourself as someone who knows how to handle money wisely, then act accordingly. Build slowly but persistently on each success. If you misstep, don't hesitate—start again. Continually reinforce the positive self-image while always acting in small ways that agree with that image. In effect, you'll be taking a stand. You'll be fulfilling your new, positive prophecy about yourself.

Taking a stand. I choose those words deliberately. Something unexpected can happen when you take a stand. You may achieve a degree of balance you've never known before. Because balance is so closely allied with my central theme—

> *Take a stand.*

living with grace and generosity—it's a subject I'll expand upon again and again. Here I wish to call attention to one of the ways we use the term in the world of dance. Common sense might lead you to think that to maintain balance while moving with a partner across a dance floor you should keep your feet parallel, weight evenly divided between them. But in reality that would lead to instability and clumsiness. Even a small push from any direction would make you waver or even fall. In actual practice the best way to "stand on your own two feet" is to favor one foot, specifically, by leading with one foot, then the other, alternating your weight back and forth as you go. At the studio we call this dancing *foot to foot*, and it's one of the first principles we teach students, starting with walking together foot to foot onto the dance floor. In life, as in dance, the best partners are those whose balance comes from leading with one foot—in other words, those who take a stand.

Balance as I'm using the term here suggests the ability to withstand forces that would otherwise slow you down, prevent you from advancing altogether, or alter your direction. Imagine a sailboat adrift on the open ocean, subject to powerful sea currents and winds that blow from all sides. How does it avoid bobbing around aimlessly like a piece of discarded Styrofoam? How does it gain control over where it goes? How, in short, does it establish direction? For one thing, the captain decides on a destination. For another, he sets the sails at an angle to the wind so that they will carry the boat toward that destination. Here's the parallel I'm drawing: The destination, which will remain constant throughout the journey, is the equivalent of a long-term goal. The angle of the sails corresponds to short-term goals, and they'll require repeated adjustment as winds and currents shift. Note that trying to resist the wind directly would cause the boat to stall or even capsize. In other words, were the captain to place the sails at a right angle to the wind, they'd be torn to shreds and the boat would be upended, maybe drowning all aboard. Instead, he turns them slightly this way and that. He neither places himself at the mercy of the wind nor bullies his way through it, foolishly trying to defy the overwhelming power of nature. Instead, he trims his sails to a position that's only slightly resistant, thereby *using* the energy of the wind to his advantage.

> Because daily circumstances shift, short-term goals require constant adjustment.

And the same thing can happen when you take a stand in everyday life, when you adopt a position in relationship to the personal, social, economic, and other winds that you're continually encountering. By making a choice, you create energy. By saying to the world that you favor this over that, you create energy. By approaching experience with a well-defined perspective, you create energy. By living with conviction, you create energy. That's the power of desire, of setting long-term goals, then setting and adjusting short-term goals as circumstances dictate so that you'll stay on course toward your long-term goals. And something else happens, something you might not associate with choice. Think of those you trust, be they lovers, friends, coworkers, or acquaintances. I'm not saying those you like. Popularity is another story. No, I'm talking about those who don't raise suspicions with you about motivation, who don't

> Living with conviction creates energy.

make you wonder where they're going to be when the going gets rough. I'll wager that most if not all of them share at least one trait: They are forthright about who they are, what they want, what they believe in, and what they value. They make decisions fairly quickly and they stick by them. You may not agree with their decisions or points of view. But you know where they stand.

I'll return to this idea in Chapter 8, which explores the dynamics of partnerships in more detail, but in the dance of life, as on the dance floor, the most promising twosomes are those in which both parties lead with one foot. If you know what you want and convey clearly to others what you want, you're far more likely to attract people who value you for who you really are, and vice versa. And you'll create trust, without which no relationship, personal or otherwise, can flourish.

We've been taught that asking for what we want is improper, rude, selfish, and so forth. And, of course, it can be if what you want is improper, rude, or selfish. But to suggest that the wanting itself is wrong is a gross misreading of how life actually works. The problem isn't desire. It's desire in the absence of grace and generosity, which leads to greed, obsession, addiction, and even violence. Being healthily engaged with the world via ambitions and convictions gives day-to-day existence an edge. It heightens the senses and increases awareness. Over time it produces a well-defined character. And though very difficult to shape consciously, character traits are the most rewarding of long-term goals because they concern not specific achievements but overall ways of going about things—who we are essentially as opposed to what we might say or do, make or acquire. I can't imagine two more desirable or constructive human traits than *grace*, or suppleness of movement, and *generosity,* the capacity to give and forgive. Both suggest largeness of spirit, which is our only lasting hope in an uncertain world, a world in which much that happens is beyond both our comprehension and our control.

> *Without grace and generosity, desire leads to greed, obsession, addiction, and violence.*

Finally, keep in mind that desire animates us, as well as the world. It keeps us curious. It makes getting up in the morning something to look forward to. In other words, it simply makes being alive much more fun. And don't forget that this is equally true of those around you. One of the greatest gifts you can give to others is to affirm them in their convictions, to offer approval when they express healthy desires. Help create a climate in which taking a stand is encouraged. Not only will this intensify experience, including making your relationships more vivid and meaningful, it will widen the overall horizon of possibility. Living with conviction will open doors you didn't know existed. Among the new prospects will be the people drawn toward you precisely because of the stands you take. When you live with

> *Help create a climate in which living with conviction is encouraged.*

conviction you become, like legendary dancer and choreographer Martha Graham says, a human magnet, and the "intensity of your own belief" attracts others. Nothing will make you more interesting as a person than being interested in the world around you. Those who are passionate about life are the most likely to arouse passion in others.

FIVE

Two Left Feet

*Filling this empty space
constitutes my identity.*

—TWYLA THARP

During the twenty-five or so years that I've been
associated with the Fred Astaire company, ballroom dancing has become increasingly popular, resulting in a dramatic shift in the makeup of our
clientele. Today we see many more couples and
young people coming through the front door than
we once did. At studios across the country there's
also been a significant increase in the number of
men who sign up for ballroom lessons, including the
so-called macho variety, who not long ago wouldn't
have set foot on a dance floor, much less allowed
their hips to sway to a salsa or rumba. But one thing
that hasn't changed is the tendency among new

enrollees to play down their abilities—and, thus, everyone's expectations, including their own. "I have two left feet" is the typical refrain. Everything our instructors do and say is aimed at putting students at ease and boosting their confidence, and it's no different in this instance when they counter with our standard response: "You're in luck. We have a closet full of right feet."

That comeback usually elicits a laugh, and it's supposed to, but it also expresses the principle that is the foundation of our entire business: Everyone can learn to dance. A parallel principle underlies this book: Everyone can learn to live well, by which I mean with grace and generosity. Let me explain by going back to the dance floor. Do some people possess greater physical ability than others? Certainly. Do some people master rhythmic movement faster or more thoroughly than others? Yes, of course. To deny such differences would be silly. But that shouldn't prevent anyone from dancing. At Fred Astaire, people in wheelchairs dance—lacking both a left foot and a right foot, you might say. One wheelchair-bound woman I know performs before public audiences in amateur exhibitions. And she puts on quite a show. What all the dancers who complete our program learn is that you needn't be perfect to have fun doing something. Much more important, *you needn't be perfect to find fulfillment.*

> *Just as everyone can learn to dance, everyone can also learn to live well.*

Perfection. What a self-destructive pursuit that can be. Let me give you an example from my own life. When I was in high school, I tried out for volleyball. I loved the game and I was pretty good, though not good enough to make the A team. But the B team, I was sure, wasn't good enough for me. Back then, I wouldn't attempt anything new unless I excelled at it from the start. So I quit. I never again played volleyball. Using my version of the "two left feet" excuse, I squandered an opportunity for enjoyment, a great deal of enjoyment, as well as a chance to improve my abilities, maybe enough to one day move up to the first squad. I'll never know because I wasn't willing to act, *to take the steps necessary to find out.* And that's what makes the episode regrettable. I turned my back on one of life's golden invitations. What I didn't realize at the time, and in fact didn't completely appreciate until years later, is that perfection is a false god, a mirage, a hindrance to living well. I needed a new way to measure the value of my life, a new, more constructive way to define my purpose, my reason for existence. And eventually I found it—in the concept of *wholeness*.

> *You needn't be perfect to lead a fulfilling life.*

These days, many therapists and self-help gurus speak of wholeness, but the person who first championed the idea was the pioneering Swiss psychologist Carl Jung. A student of Sigmund Freud, Jung developed an approach that differed fundamentally from that of his teacher. Whereas Freud stressed the negative impact of childhood experience, Jung emphasized the positive effects of integrating all experience, which he believed necessary if one is to develop into a well-rounded individual. This is an almost cartoonish version of two brilliant psychological systems, but it highlights what's useful for our purposes. Jung said that we achieve psychological well-being by accepting all aspects of the self. He encouraged men to embrace their feminine side, for instance, and women to embrace their masculine side, and everyone to recognize and integrate their dark side.

Striving for perfection, especially as it's commonly practiced, would have struck Jung as a form of insanity. Even if perfection were possible, and it's not, the typical way people try to achieve it is the psychological equivalent of mutilating oneself—cutting ourselves off from undesirable elements in our character. To grasp the error in this all-too-common "solution" to personal troubles, imagine a teenage girl taking ballet lessons. She's attempting to perform a plié, bending her knees with her legs turned out, which usually is the first exercise in ballet training. But her left leg isn't quite as strong as her right. She loses balance, wobbles. Should she cut off the offending leg?

No, of course not. The question is absurd. But equally absurd is the attempt to ignore, renounce, or otherwise refuse to acknowledge aspects of ourselves that for some reason don't measure up. The aspiring ballet dancer should practice moving both legs in unison, which requires that she strengthen the weaker of the two. Likewise, we should practice getting the various facets of our entire being moving in unison, which requires that we find ways to make peace with troublesome parts of ourselves. Why? Because the only way to gain control over something is by making

> *Striving for perfection causes psychological damage, but striving for wholeness brings fulfillment.*

it your own. That's why striving for wholeness, as Jung prescribed, is superior to striving for perfection. To be whole is to be fulfilled as a human being. If that seems a little fuzzy, try thinking of it this way: During a single lifetime, each person is allotted a certain amount of space within which to grow, create, and experience. Let's call

> *Your task as a human being is to fill up your life space, to use the whole dance floor.*

it the individual's *life space*. Now picture your life space as a personal dance floor. It's impossible to know beforehand the size and shape of your dance floor, in other words, the limits to what's possible for you to achieve during the course of your life. You discover the limits to your life space only by doing, by acting, by actually getting out on the floor and moving. Your task as a human being is to fill up your life space, to use the whole dance floor. The closer you get to doing that, the more fulfilled you'll be.

Earlier I spoke of fear in terms of the discouragement and disapproval we encounter as we grow from childhood to adulthood and how those negative experiences can become internalized as a subversive, sometimes paralyzing inner voice: the critic. This sad metamorphosis is usually so slow that it's virtually impossible to detect, but the results are the same— self-doubt, withdrawal, defensiveness—and most of us are affected to one degree or another. Now I want to approach fear from a different direction, using the concept of wholeness to explore how to overcome obstacles to fulfillment. The first step, of

> *Pretending you're not fearful makes you a slave to fear.*

course, is to admit that under certain circumstances you are fearful. This is easier to do if you keep in mind that you're not alone; you don't have a corner on fear. It's a universal emotion. In fact, fear is as natural as breathing. And it's been around almost as long.

According to evolutionary biologists, what we call fear is a set of physiological processes—increased heart rate, a surge of adrenaline, heightened senses, and so on—that *Homo sapiens* developed to deal with threats and crises. And the processes culminate in one of two basic responses: fight or flight. When a ferocious saber-toothed tiger attacked one of your prehistoric ancestors, his only hope for survival was to disable the tiger or somehow escape. The threats we face today are different, of course. Instead of angry tigers, we contend with angry bosses, spouses, and creditors. But our responses remain the same. Do you doubt that? Pay close attention the next time you're really scared. I guarantee that you'll feel an adrenaline-fueled urge to attack or run away—most likely, to run away. Fear, in other words, can be useful. At times it's even essential to survival. In its most basic form, fear protects us from harm, as does our ability to feel pain. Imagine how much damage we'd do to ourselves, for example, were we unable to sense the heat radiating from a hot stove. Illogical as it might seem, our sensitivity to the world around us, including other people, is a type of

> *Fear can be useful, by protecting us from real harm.*

strength. Or as I like to put it, vulnerability isn't a four-letter word.

As with all attempts to deny or suppress unpleasant emotions, pretending that you're not scared requires energy. That's why simply admitting fear can be liberating in itself. At Fred Astaire I see this all the time, especially among first-time students. While waiting for instruction to begin, they become increasingly uneasy, with all the tell-tale signs. Their muscles constrict, their breathing accelerates, their attention wanders, and they fidget. In other words, they exhibit the classic fight-or-flight reaction. But dancing requires precisely the opposite: relaxed muscles; slow, evenly paced breathing; focused awareness; and smooth movement. Tense people are difficult to teach.

More important for you, tense people find it difficult to learn.

Admitting fear is liberating.

So instructors try to get students to acknowledge that they may be a little uptight, intimidated. They do this by using humor, offering various kinds of reassurance, displaying a calm demeanor of their own, and so on. At the same time—and this is crucial—they convey that in fact there's nothing on the dance floor to fear. To dance is to play. And what's so scary about play? The power of this prescription comes from combining two seemingly contradictory messages: *Yes, your fear is real. But it's no big deal because there's nothing real to fear.* Applied to the dance floor of life, this approach has the effect of helping you reclaim unwanted parts of yourself, which is necessary to achieve wholeness. It can also help you realize that much of your fearfulness isn't attached to real threats. It can help you identify those of your fears that have a life of their own, independent of any particular circumstances.

What I mean by fears taking on a life of their own is that they've become habitual. Have you ever seen a dog that was repeatedly mistreated when it was a puppy? Maybe it mopes along with its tail tucked between its legs and its head hanging down. Maybe it cowers or whimpers whenever someone extends a hand to pet it. Maybe it avoids people, hiding or running away at the first sign of a stranger. All of these behaviors are indications that the animal's normal way of dealing with potentially stressful situations has been damaged or distorted. After being exposed to excessive threats, its fight-or-flight response is too easily triggered or, worse still, the switch stays on all the time, regardless of what may be happening in its environment. The dog can no longer tell the difference between friend and foe, between a benign gesture and a malicious one, reacting to all encounters as if they were certain to be harmful. Such an unfortunate creature has made a habit of being fearful, a habit that can be hard to break.

The everyday fear that human beings display isn't nearly so pronounced, of course, nor so crippling. But the process by which fear gains the upper hand is similar. More important, so is the result. The circumstances that trigger the fear can vary greatly, but inside every inappropriately fearful person is the equivalent of a cowering, quivering animal. What can be done about it? For starters, as I described in Chapter 3, it's just about impossible to break the fear habit without reducing the influence of the inner critic. And that's achieved, you might recall, by taking small steps despite or in defiance of the critic's nonstop criticism, developing an alternative internal voice that contradicts the critic, and surrounding yourself with people who will also serve as a counterpoint, refusing to allow you to succumb to your inner critic and instead bringing out the best in you. I call this *creating your own cheering section.* I understand that this advice will strike some people as an exercise in self-delusion. I also appreciate that it's easy to confuse the idea of a self-made cheering section with a Pollyannaish belief in what's traditionally been known as "the power of positive thinking." But believe me, it works. Not in the sense that you can bend the world to your wishes, which *is* delusional, but in the sense that you can marshal the courage and develop the concentration necessary to make the most of what the world offers you—fulfilling yourself by filling up your life space.

> *To reduce the power of negative emotions, create your own cheering section.*

By now you've certainly noticed that after introducing key themes and images I return to them now and again, but each time in a slightly modified way, elaborating upon their meaning and implications. A good example is increasing awareness, which I've already mentioned as the first step in learning how to live well. Such repetition is very much in keeping with the spirit of dance, as well as of music in general. Each dance consists of certain basic moves; each musical composition, of certain movements. What distinguishes one tango from another, for instance, is how a couple varies the basic moves and how they arrange the variations as the dance progresses. In the same way, it seems to me the basic moves of life, starting with birth and including such fundamentals as falling in love, forming friendships, and taking care of others, are common to everyone. The difference, and it makes all the difference in the world, comes from *how* we execute life's basic moves and *when* in the course of a lifetime the moves are most fitting and most fruitful. It's all approach and timing.

Both approach and timing figure prominently in any attempt to reduce the influence of fear. We've been talking about approach, so let's now turn to timing. Once you start paying closer attention to when and where negative emotions arise, you'll discover that habitual fear is fear that's out of sync with circumstance. It's fear in the absence of danger or that's out of proportion to a specific danger. Don't forget my earlier remarks. I'm not suggesting that the emotion is unreal. Nor is it entirely without basis. What I'm saying is that habitual fear arises from a misreading of one's environment. Except in extreme cases, when a person loses touch with reality altogether, what usually happens is that certain aspects of a situation remind us of an earlier unpleasant experience, like a note that reverberates after a guitar string is plucked, or like the roar that probably resounded in your ancestor's ears long after the saber-toothed tiger disappeared. When we hear the echo, we nonetheless react as if we were hearing the original sound. The echo can be loud, as when a man's energetic but essentially harmless manner reminds a woman of her *aggressive* and abusive ex-boyfriend, or faint, as when the mere

> *Like all habitual emotions, habitual fear is fear that's out of sync with circumstance.*

fact that an experience is *new* is reminiscent of previous occasions when one tried something for the first time and was punished, humiliated, or otherwise discouraged.

Notice that awareness applies to both internal and external elements. Be mindful of what's going on within yourself, acknowledging when negative emotions appear. Are your muscles tight, your mind racing? Is it because you're fearful—literally, filling up with fear? But also be alert to what's actually taking place in your environment. When you look around the room, look carefully. Do you see a tiger? Are you really in danger? Personal growth depends as much on unlearning bad habits as it does on learning good ones, and it's no different here. Remember that the topic of this chapter is awkwardness, imperfection, the stumbles, blunders, and missteps that are unavoidable if you're going to learn how to walk, to dance, to live fully. The reason I'm giving so much attention to fear is that stumbling as such is neither good nor bad. It's simply a fact of life. But we complicate and confuse matters needlessly by developing an attitude toward stumbling that's self-defeating. By the time we reach adulthood, the negative emotions aroused by the mere *possibility* of stumbling— fear, embarrassment, withdrawal, defensiveness, even anger toward others—are so deeply ingrained that it's a wonder we're capable of placing one foot in front of the other. And precisely because habitual negative emotions are so much a part of who we are, and thus mistaken for something natural or necessary,

> Personal growth depends as much on unlearning bad habits as it does on learning good ones.

unlearning cannot occur without first recognizing what needs to be unlearned.

A very smart French philosopher once observed that all of humankind's misfortunes can be traced to an inability to sit still. That was almost four hundred years ago. Since then the world has become more frenetic, people more restless. Being still, slowing down and reconnecting with the here-and-now, is more difficult than ever. And it's also more necessary than ever. There's scarcely an American alive today who wouldn't benefit from stepping off his or her personal treadmill. Try it. Set aside some time each day to do nothing—and, more important, to do it well. The first thing you'll discover, of course, is that doing nothing is difficult, maybe impossible. You may be able to sit in one place for a short time, but your mind will continue to race. You'll roam aimlessly from past to future and back again, anywhere but the present. Let yourself roam. See where it takes you. If you practice being still often enough and long enough, you'll find that the interior circus quiets down. You'll also find yourself drawn to certain past experiences, lingering emotions, imaginary scenes, any of which may make you uneasy. Welcome the uneasiness, as well. Watch it come; then watch it go. While touring your mental landscape, tell yourself that you're more than everything you see and hear. But allow what wants to be seen and heard to emerge, no matter how painful or alarming it might be, because that's precisely when you're getting close to the truth of your existence.

> *Set aside some time each day to do nothing—and to do it well.*

What I've just described—*doing nothing well*—goes by a more familiar name, of course: meditation. And while I'm far from an expert on the subject, I do know that regularly practicing one of the many well-established methods for calming oneself is also an excellent way to increase self-awareness (see Chapter 14 for a list of meditation resources). I also know that exploring what other religions or cultures have to offer doesn't require one to give up one's own convictions. You can borrow a technique without buying the spiritual message that sometimes, but not always, accompanies it. Keep in mind that some form of meditation is practiced in *every* major religion, including certain highly refined prayer traditions in Christianity. Also keep in mind that in all its forms meditation has served the same practical purpose for hundreds, even thousands of years—helping people find peace of mind. I don't know anyone who doesn't need more of that. And I'll bet that includes you, too. Am I wrong?

Regardless of the method one uses for achieving stillness, and it doesn't have to be mediation as such, my point here is that sometimes you have to step back, to take a deep breath, before you step out on the dance floor of life. Reducing the influence of habitual fear is easier if you've been practicing being aware and gradually developing a counter-habit of allowing all feelings, including fear, to flow through you unimpeded. You're then more likely to not compound a challenging situation by pretending you feel differently than you really do. The energy that's freed up when you cease denying fear often is just enough to enable you to

> *Shrug off the missteps and keep moving, always moving.*

take the first scary step to fulfillment, as well as to take a second step, and a third, even when they're sometimes missteps. This is how *attention*, or being mindful of yourself and your surroundings, is converted into *intention*—summoning

> ~⟨
> *Use attention to develop intention.*

the strength to act on your deepest desires. And if you happen to experience a temporary loss of nerve, a hesitation, don't interpret it as anything more than another form of stumbling. Just shrug it off and keep moving. Finally, always bring your cheering section, even if it's nothing more than the voice you've created to counter that nagging inner critic: *Trying is succeeding. Persistence is beauty. Seek fulfillment, not perfection. Life belongs to those who want it the most—those who keep moving across the dance floor no matter how often they stumble.*

None of this is easy, I admit. And setbacks are to be expected. More than that, if you've followed what I've been saying, you'll realize that setbacks are part of the process. They're as much a part of the dance of life as achievements.

> ~⟨
> *By avoiding pain, you also risk avoiding joy.*

Fear isn't the only negative emotion that can take on a life of its own, preventing one from reaching fulfillment. But it's the most common—among dancers and among people in general. Fear of failure, fear of humiliation, fear of rejection. All very real, yes. And when they become habitual, all can be based on a grave misunderstanding about how life actually works.

During those special times when I've been able to find a still point from which to observe what's going on around me, one thing that always becomes clear is that life is rhythmic. It really is a dance. Like the sea, it rises and falls. Like the weather, it turns round and round, transforming from one season to another, then another, then starting all over again. The ebb and flow, the never-ending cycles—these are fundamental characteristics of life on Earth. We have no choice in the matter. They're beyond our control.

How amusing, pathetic, and ultimately self-sabotaging it is that we so often convince ourselves that this isn't so, acting instead as if we're in charge of and responsible for the ebb and flow of life. Avoiding trouble and the pain it brings is as likely to be successful as attempting to turn back the tide. In a very real sense, life *is* trouble. If not that, it's at least *troublesome*. What this means on an everyday level is that problems will always come and go, just as everything else comes and goes. Recognize that, truly accept that, and you'll discover that your troubles, big and small, are easier to face. In other words, don't make the unavoidable problems of existence worse, sometimes much worse, by denying that problems should exist in the first place. That's a waste of energy. So is attempting to control the broader currents of one's life so as to sidestep problems altogether.

Another common way we waste precious energy is trying to solve problems that don't have solutions or, putting it differently, treating unavoidable aspects of the ebb and flow of life as if they were things that can be fixed. What do I mean by that? Maybe another example from the dance world will make it clearer. If you've witnessed professional ballroom dancers competing, you know how intense such contests can be—emotionally as well as physically. Simply because the couples are highly skilled and experienced doesn't mean they're free from fear, self-doubt, embarrassment, or any of the other potentially destructive feelings that plague those new to the dance floor. Indeed, as a consequence of the intensity, especially the intense desire to do well, combined with the fact that only one couple can place first, competitive dancers constantly experience rejection, which could easily undo them if they adopted the wrong attitude. Rejection, as it happens, isn't a "problem" that can be remedied but instead is a necessary part of the process. To not make the cut for the next round of competition, for example, is for professionals what not making the right move is for amateurs. It's another form of stumbling, another kind of imperfection. Likewise, it must be taken in stride—neither feared nor regretted.

Were a dancer at any level, whether novice or veteran, to make a habit of fear or regret, he or she would stop improving the skills, if not cease dancing altogether. He or she would become too paralyzed to risk the next step. Similarly, in the dance of life, if we allowed our fear of making mistakes or our humiliation over having made mistakes to dictate how we behave, we'd remain fixed in place. Worst of all, our hearts would close. We'd become estranged from the world, cut off from the ebb and flow of life—from the very things that give life meaning and make fulfillment possible. Despite the consequences, of course, most of us will be tempted to withdraw from the dance floor, at least temporarily, and most of us will yield to the temptation. And we'll continue to yield until we realize that by treating what's necessary as something optional we're squandering our birthright. Certain problems present themselves again and again and again, in one form after another, until we wake up and absorb what they have to teach us.

> *Some problems will continue to present themselves until we learn what they have to teach us.*

If nothing else convinces us of the foolishness of not trying, not getting out on the dance floor, maybe this will: By avoiding pain you also risk avoiding joy. That's the price of never knowing joy. Quite a toll, wouldn't you say? Yet some people, most people, are willing to pay that toll at least some of the time. I confess that there have been occasions when I've been willing to pay it. I'm not proud of those moments. And afterward I've always regretted

> *It's far better to dance with two left feet than not to dance at all.*

succumbing to fear and self-doubt. It's far better to dance with two left feet than not to dance at all. Indeed, that's one way to look at life—dancing with two left feet. And the wonder is how graceful two left feet can be, if only they're allowed to be.

SIX

Energy in Motion

The body is a sacred garment.
It's your first and last garment . . .
and it should be treated with honor.

—MARTHA GRAHAM

Remember the personal epiphany I referred to back in the first chapter—recognizing how much of my life I was devoting to work and therefore realizing the urgent need to cultivate work relationships that are as healthy and productive as possible? That led to an entirely different management philosophy. The hallmarks of the philosophy are the same concepts that underpin this book: (1) significant human change usually occurs within the context of relationships and (2) all relationships function according to the same basic dynamics. By dynamics I mean the ways that energy is created and destroyed, how energy moves, and the manner in which energy is transformed within an individual, as well as transferred from one individual to another. This perspective comes naturally to a dancer because the essence of dance is energy. Or, to put it differently: Dancing, like all forms of physical activity, is an expression of energy; it's energy that assumes recognizable shapes—such as the quick-step, fox-trot, and so forth—and which evolves over time. *Energy in motion*. When I ran Fred Astaire Dance Studios in Phoenix, I made the most of this fact, even in my relationships with employees, using a resource that most people in supervisory positions lack—the dance floor itself. Allow me to explain.

The essence of dance is energy.

During the routine operations of any group, be it a family, social organization, or business, communication can break down at any time. So can decision-making, problem-solving, or any other function essential to the group's vitality and longevity. Every manager has experienced this. A crisis occurs. You consider it from all angles but no solution presents itself. You've reached an impasse. You feel stuck—literally, fixed in place, incapable of moving forward. This usually is a good time to step back, take a deep breath, and pay very close attention to the crisis itself rather than blindly and reflexively trying to resolve it. In short, find or create a still point amid the storm and simply watch what's happening around you. Where exactly is the impasse located? What is the nature of the impasse—exactly? Who's in a position to do something about it? And what might that something be? Exactly?

Because I'm in a people business rather than a product

business, I often found that the impasse resided in, you guessed it, people. Specifically, one or another of the staff members who worked for me. Though the impasses they caused might seriously disrupt certain studio operations, often the source turned out to be not so serious, such as a lackluster attitude following a sleepless night or sense of failure for not having performed a minor task properly. My response varied depending on circumstances, but sometimes I handled such "crises" by telling the staff member to dance it off. That's right. *Dance it off.* Work it out of her system through dancing. I was dead serious. And more often than not the depressed or distracted party returned from the dance floor in better spirits, ready to resume work and to do so with confidence and determination.

The reason is simple and I've already revealed it: The essence of dance is energy. If you don't feel the energy before you take your first step, you almost certainly will after you've twirled across the floor a few times. Motion can alter the mind. Under the right conditions, it releases magical chemicals called endorphins, the naturally occurring mood elevators in the brain. Now you know why we also end student dance sessions with Latin numbers, such as sambas and cha-chas, highly energetic dances that invariably make people feel better. We don't consider our lessons successful unless our clients leave the studio jazzed up, glad to be who they are (at least for the time being), and ready to take on the next challenge. That makes the parallel between dance and life pretty obvious, doesn't it? Energy, you see, is also the essence of life. By consistently applying this principle to your day-to-day existence

> ⟋◌
> *Motion
> alters the mind.*

you can develop a powerful new tool for self-actualization, one that will serve you well for the rest of your days. Just as your attitude, emotions, and overall disposition register in your body—tense muscles, for instance, or stiff joints—so too can what you do with your muscles and joints influence your mental state. In other words, you can be moved (in the psychological sense) by physical movement.

But the key is physical movement. Energy in motion. Earlier I puzzled over the transformation that occurs in almost all of us, by which the lightheartedness we know as children is gradually replaced by heaviness of spirit. The most extreme of the heavy spirits are easy to spot—by their sluggishness, low motivation, avoidance of new experiences, as well as attributes like poor posture and discolored skin. Often their eyes are dull. Their faces lack radiance. Their voices are flat, constricted, or strained. Heavy spirits tend to age prematurely or, perhaps more precisely, tend to take on the manner and appearance of aging earlier in life than need be. Excessive weight gain can also be a symptom of a heavy spirit, but not every heavy person is a heavy spirit. One of the greatest rewards of being a dance instructor is helping a large individual move in ways that she or he never imagined possible or, fearing ridicule, never dared attempt. Their lightness of being on the dance floor is a kind of everyday poetry and an inspiration to all who witness it, seasoned dance professionals included.

I want to dwell on the last example for a moment. After observing people of all ages, backgrounds, and physical types successfully learning how to ballroom dance, I've come to be-lieve that one of the most underrated aspects of our emotional life is the destructive role of humiliation. Sometimes I think it's even more funda-mental than love, at least in the sense that self-respect and the respect of others are necessary to maintain identity, and in the absence of identity almost everything

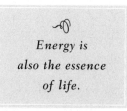

Energy is
also the essence
of life.

else we need to fulfill ourselves as human beings, including giv-ing and receiving love, is nearly impossible. To be loved or to be in love, you first have to *be* someone.

Humiliation and the fear of humiliation erode identity. If prolonged, they'll all but dissolve it. And once you lose your identity, you lose your appetite for life, your will to live. This is why the madmen who ran the concentration camps during World War II devised insidious methods for stripping human beings of all trappings of self-respect, from removing all their personal belongings, to making them live with filth, disease, and starvation, to forcing them to witness or partake in the deaths of their children, spouses, or parents. Their goal was to destroy the identity of their captives and thereby achieve total dominance over them. That they failed so often, even after months of torment and degradation, is a resounding testament to the resilience and immense potential of the human spirit.

Morally speaking, light years separate the horrors of these concentration camps in the 1940s from the innocent atmosphere of dance floors in contemporary America. But there's another aspect of that most extreme of cases that deserves considera-tion because of its implications for ordinary life today. Recall

what I said about control toward the end of the last chapter—
that it's foolish to try to control the ebb and flow of life. I admit
that that's a little abstract. So let me try to clarify what I meant
by making an important distinction. If you examine fear closely
what you often find fueling it is a desire for control. The rookie
dancer who dreads stumbling is in fact afraid of losing
control—of his body, his surroundings, even his life. On a psychological level, surprising as it may seem, all of that can be at
stake even when tackling something as frivolous or innocuous
as dancing. That's how fundamental self-respect is to our overall approach to the world. Although the aim of dance instructors is to persuade students to overcome their fears, their
self-doubt, what they actually say is
this: *Let go*. Let go of expectation, anticipation, anything and everything that
makes you hesitate. Replace thinking
with doing. Get your worries out of your
head. In a word, *move!* Whether you're conscious of it or not,
what this requires is giving up control. To master dancing—or,
for that matter, any new skill—you have to surrender yourself
to it.

> *Surrender
> to the dance.*

Okay, here comes that distinction, and it amounts to another paradox: Just as all of us need love, a sense of accomplishment, value to others, and belongingness, we also need to
feel effective and to be able to influence the world in which we
live. The word I used before was efficacy, which, of course, is a
fancy way of saying control. And I stand by that assertion: A
certain amount of control is necessary for psychological well-
being. Losing control is humiliating. It destroys confidence, it

saps strength, it crushes the will. Hence, the techniques of the concentration camp, which were meant to make the inmates feel entirely at the mercy of the cruel whims of their captors. The trick is achieving the right balance, specifically, recognizing what lies beyond one's control, an idea memorably embodied in the well-known Serenity Prayer. Written by the American theologian Reinhold Niebuhr but most strongly associated with Alcoholics Anonymous and other so-called twelve-step programs, the prayer asks God to grant the supplicant "the serenity to accept the things [he] cannot change; courage to change the things [he] can; and wisdom to know the difference." What the prayer overlooks, however, is that sometimes the only way to "know the difference" is to test the limits. Such wisdom isn't something you possess ahead of time; it's what you acquire by taking action and thereby discovering what's possible—by filling your life space and every once in a while bumping up against the boundaries.

To gain mastery of anything new, you must first own up to incompetence, ignorance.

The paradox is that testing the limits of an unfamiliar situation usually requires you to temporarily give up the all-too-human desire to be in charge. To achieve mastery you must first own up to your incompetence, your ignorance. Pretending that you know what you don't know will prevent you from learning because that sort of deception wastes energy and diverts attention, and learning won't take place in the absence of properly focused energy. If instead you surrender yourself, you'll soon enough find that you're also enlarging yourself, that you're achieving fulfillment. But you must be willing to be childlike again, to be playful, open-minded, curious, and, most important, willing to make mistakes, which isn't easy for some adults. This interplay of surrender and control will come up again in later chapters—regarding romantic partnerships, responsibility to others and for others, and profound loss. For the rest of this chapter, though, I want to explore how the interplay applies to physical movement, in particular, the extent to which action is the representation of thought and thought is the consequence of action—a self-reinforcing circle that can be either creative or destructive.

Students and teachers alike frequently make a comment that sheds light on the relationship between mind and body. They say that when they get on the dance floor, whatever pain they may have been experiencing beforehand either disappears or simply doesn't matter as much. Having on many occasions competed when exhausted, injured, depressed, or broken-hearted, I know exactly what they mean. Dancing at its best, when you feel free to close your eyes and give yourself to the rhythm and motion, is pure joy. Small wonder that so many people, regardless of their level of skill, find it addictive. Nor is it a surprise that in recent years dancing has become a popular alternative to the drudgery of conventional exercise. What more and more Americans of all ages are discovering is that dancing is an excellent way to improve fitness, and not just physical fitness.

Dancing
is pure joy.

The secret of dancing's appeal is, of course, that it's more fun than most of the activities available at the local gym. Dancing tends to be seen as play; it doesn't have the negative connotations of the standard "workout." And every fitness trainer will tell you that you're more likely to continue exercising if you actually enjoy the exercise activity you choose to do on a regular basis. What may surprise you is the range of benefits that can be derived from this particular form of play. Research has shown that ballroom dancers burn from 250 to 400 calories per hour. The more energetic the dance—West Coast swing, rumba, and so on—the more pronounced the training effect. John O'Hurley, the immensely likable actor who performed so well on the 2005 *Dancing with the Stars* television series, reportedly lost twenty pounds during his time on the show. Still more encouraging, a recent experiment conducted in Italy found that the cardiovascular benefits of three weekly dance sessions lasting about twenty minutes each equal those of a similar regimen on a bicycle or treadmill. Besides being aerobic—accelerating your breathing and blood flow—dancing is isometric, meaning that it improves muscle tone, specifically because of the emphasis on proper posture and coordination, as well as the constant movement of arms, legs, and torso. Often this translates into stress relief, as well, helping to relax clenched shoulders and relieve neck tension.

Although to dance well you must *get your worries out of your head*—stop thinking about making mistakes—it's a complex physical activity that still requires a certain amount of mental concentration. You have to follow the beat of the music. You have to pay attention to where you place your feet and when.

And often you have to be able to carry on a conversation with your partner at the same time. Much, in short, is happening during even the most routine of tangos, and your brain is co-ordinating all of it. For some time now, it's been known that routinely engaging in brain-challenging activities reduces the risk of developing dementia. Use it or lose it, as the adage goes. But a study in New York, completed only a few years ago, went even further, demonstrating that reading, playing a musical in-strument, and similar cognitive pursuits make it less likely that one will be afflicted by the worst form of dementia—Alzheimer's disease. Dancing several times a week can cut the chances by a whopping 75 percent. Add these mental benefits to the aerobic and isometric effects, the surge of mood-elevating chemicals in the brain, and the overall pleasure that comes from social interaction with people whose company you enjoy, and we've found a physical activity that does it all. Never did play work so many wonders for the whole human being.

> *Dance works wonders for the whole human being.*

That's a biased remark, I confess. Dancing certainly isn't the only physical activity that both honors the "sacred garment"—Martha Graham's lovely term for the body—and stimulates the mind. But it may well be the most convenient and easiest to master for ordinary people. That said, the idea I wish to convey here is that regardless of differences in taste and accessibility, some kind of regular physical activity is essential to living well. And because most of us lead largely sedentary lives, remaining faithful to the activity that best suits us usually requires a conscious effort, especially after we take on the obligations of family, job, and community. It was a lot easier for me to jog or in-line skate five days a week before I got married. Each of us must find his or her own way of resolving this dilemma, I'm afraid. And if we're just getting started, or starting again, we also have to muster up enough stamina to endure the first stage, which can be long on punishment and short on reward.

> *Choose a physical activity you truly enjoy.*

I wish I could offer a magic formula, but there isn't one, and never will be, just as there will never be a magic formula for losing weight, other than eating less and doing more. I can only reiterate what the fitness experts advise: Choose a physical activity you truly enjoy. You're more likely to stick with it—to dance through the pain—and make it an indispensable part of your overall lifestyle.

Besides spending far too much time on our backsides, virtually immobile, another regrettable feature of contemporary life is an increasing alienation from the natural world. As recently as two hundred years ago, most Americans didn't have to pack their cars and travel long distances to be able to experience nature. They lived in natural settings, or very close by, on farms and ranches, in small towns separated by long stretches of hills, prairie, desert, mountains. Back then, all this was well-known and duly appreciated: the changing seasons; the cycle of life and death; the interdependence of living things, including our reliance on other plants and animals for survival; the life-sustaining role of such basic elements as water, air, earth, and fire; and the untamable heart of the nonhuman world.

Trading that intimate relationship with nature for the man-made amenities of urban and suburban existence has come at a steep price: an increasing inability to recognize and, most important, respect the ebb and flow of life.

Our lack of sensitivity and respect extends to that part of the natural world with which we should be most intimate—our own bodies. This is an ironic situation, as well as a fortunate one, because it means that a remedy to our alienation from nature is at hand. Literally. It's in our fingers, toes, arms, and legs. It's in every gesture, every motion, the transformations we undergo as we grow and age, the cycles of hunger and satiation, sexual arousal and sexual fulfillment, falling asleep and waking up. Most of all, it's in the rhythmic beating of our hearts and the cadences of breathing. In dancing we pay particular attention to breathing because it's a strong indicator of a person's state of being—mentally and physically. Rapid shallow breathing, for instance, usually reflects tension, constriction. People who aren't comfortable in their own skin, who are locked up emotionally, tend to take short, shallow breaths. But because of the special relationship between mind and body, we can reverse this dynamic, using breathing techniques to put people at ease and free them from such paralyzing emotions as fear and self-doubt. By calming the body, you can calm the mind, too.

> *Calm the mind by calming the body.*

When I was an instructor, I'd tell new students to close their eyes and focus on the bodily sensations they experienced as they turned across the dance floor. *Let go of your thoughts and simply surrender yourself to the movement.* And because I'd worked hard on building trust, they tried to oblige, often awkwardly at first, and often having to stop, then start again, and yet again. But in time, and with persistence, everyone underwent a transformation, and it was less a function of improved skill than increased composure. They stepped bravely over the threshold that separates embarrassment from fulfillment. No longer did they worry about making mistakes, which in turn enabled them to direct all of their attention to the dance itself. And here's the most important feature of all: They tapped into a reservoir of energy they scarcely knew existed. The students became lighter, livelier, as if they might at any moment ascend from the dance floor and take flight. And the effect continued afterward. Their walk was freer, more open. They expressed enthusiasm and confidence. Their faces beamed.

> *Step over the threshold from embarrassment to fulfillment.*

Anyone who's experienced this, through dancing or some other exhilarating physical activity, knows that the pleasure it provides is a powerful incentive to continue, to return for more. The senses come alive. Sensation is intensified. Energy courses through your body, making you feel electrified, increasing your appetite for all that life has to offer. And at that very moment you realize, even if you don't have the words to express it, that the wild heart of existence is in fact beating inside your chest. The natural world is as much within you as it is out there, beyond the city limits, at the end of the pavement. Also at that moment you may realize that it's possible to achieve harmony between the cadences of your day-to-day behavior and the broader currents of existence, which is the highest form of respect—for oneself as well as for the irreplaceable gift that is life. You can flow with the Flow.

What I have in mind when I say, *"flow with the Flow,"* might be easier to grasp if I introduce the idea of *phrasing,* which in ballroom dancing refers to the relative match between specific dance moves, or figures, and the rhythm and melody of the music being played. Proper phrasing dictates that certain steps and turns, for example, coincide with certain beats or act as a counterpoint to certain beats. To sustain proper phrasing during a long, complicated dance routine requires not only the ability to perform each of the figures but also the ability to perform one figure after another in time with the music and without stopping to rest. If you're in poor physical condition, this will be difficult if not impossible. It will seem as if you're trying to swim upstream. If, on the other hand, you've built up your stamina through practice, the sensation can be precisely the reverse. It then feels like you've aligned yourself with some outside source of energy, that you're traveling with the current instead of against it. You're in sync, you're in the groove. What once was laborious is now effortless. The spirit of the dance has entered you—it's dancing through you. Your movements and the movement of the music are one. And that's flowing with the Flow.

Something similar can happen off the dance floor, and again the key is movement, movement in the broadest sense—the rhythms and cycles and overall direction of your life. From one

> To flow with the flow requires presence and a keen sense of timing.

moment to the next, from one experience to the other. If you're familiar with self-help language, you've probably run across the admonition "be present in the moment." It's sound advice, backed up by spiritual traditions that have stood the test of time. My version goes like this: *Be present as you move from one moment to the next.* I want to stress an active approach to life, as well as the importance of aligning your "figures" with the ebb and flow of the world around you. Nothing is more moving than being moved by a spirit larger than yourself, and that's most likely to occur when you're fully present—your attention focused on the here-and-now—during the properly timed ex-pression of energy, be it dancing, work-ing, loving, or taking care of others. This is your best hope for achieving a measure of grace, when each moment flows into the next as harmoniously as the notes in a brilliant musical composition. It's also your best hope for fulfillment, reaching

> *Be present*
> *as you move*
> *from moment*
> *to moment.*

those singular moments when all that you have done before-hand comes to fruition. Life gives most people the opportunity to experience many such moments. We have but to set aside our fears and join the dance.

SEVEN

Dancing Solo

*Many people have asked me
if I have a favorite role, to which
I answer that my favorite role is
the one I am dancing now.*

—MARTHA GRAHAM

A popular (and amusing) observation about ballroom dancing is that it's more difficult for women because they're wearing high heels and always moving backward. But picture being in heels and going through all of the motions, including the backward ones, of a complex ballroom dance *without a partner*. I first saw this happen many years ago, when a highly experienced professional couple performed in a public dance showcase. During such exhibitions, dancers are free from the pressure they normally experience in competitive settings. And since there are no rules governing which dances they perform or how they do so, they have greater latitude to innovate. The resulting playful atmosphere can lead to impressive displays of physical strength and agility, often involving the woman assuming extreme positions of one kind or another. And that's what made the professional couple's exhibition all the more amazing. The show began with the woman walking alone onto the dance floor, then performing an entire number by herself—exactly as she would were she actually dancing with her partner. Then the man joined her and they danced the same routine together.

Imagine a film about a pair of dancers, perhaps a couple you've seen on a television program, such as *Dancing with the Stars* or *America's Ballroom Challenge*. They're dancing a waltz, the fox trot, or the dramatic Spanish number known as the pase doble. The couple turns, twists, slides, bends. They're constantly in motion, constantly in harmony, and every step flows gracefully into the next. Now wind the film back to the beginning, remove the man, then watch the woman perform the very same turns and bends on her own. Arm placement, the position of the feet, the angle of the head: Everything is duplicated in precise detail. As you might guess, this is an exercise that requires an enormous amount of practice, not to mention a great sense of balance. And witnessing it is exhilarating. Audiences routinely erupt in applause, largely because of the skills being displayed, but also because it's unusual in professional ballroom dancing for a woman to perform by herself, and it never happens for more than a few seconds. To see a woman dancing solo and doing it exceptionally well, without the support of a partner, is a rare pleasure. It's also an inspiration to all female dancers.

I must explain that, among seasoned professional dancers, both the man and the woman should be capable of performing their routines solo, even though they'll never actually be called upon to do so, at least not in competition. Another way of saying this is that they should know their respective parts so thoroughly that neither relies on the other to carry them through the routines. Because each partner has achieved balance as a separate individual, the overall partnership also is balanced. Most important, the dance is balanced. I learned this the hard way early in my career as a ballroom dancer. Michael, my partner, easily memorized our choreographed routines. I didn't. Not at first. During rehearsals, I would lose my way, which forced me to lean on him for guidance, when it didn't disrupt the dance altogether. Not surprisingly, Michael grew increasingly frustrated, while I became increasingly embarrassed, which can be an explosive mix. One day, after I botched a move, he stopped abruptly and declared, "Okay, that's it. You dance your part by yourself until you know it."

> *When each partner achieves balance as an individual, the overall partnership is more likely to be balanced.*

I was so upset that I started to cry. We were supposed to be practicing *together*. And now Michael wanted me to practice *alone*? What good would that do? Eventually, however, I put aside my negative emotions and tried dancing the routine entirely on my own. I've never felt more awkward nor more self-conscious. Nor had it ever been clearer how much work I needed to do to learn my routines. I quickly discovered that I'd been relying on Michael even more than I thought. This is a mistake that's easy for women to make, I think, because on the dance floor the man is always expected to take the lead. What was needed now was for me to shift perspective, to dance without anyone else's guidance. And it worked. Once I learned a routine alone, I learned it for life. From that day onward, I incorporated solitary practice as a training tool, with both amateurs and professionals. My decision was confirmed when a European trainer held an advanced workshop at the studio in which he stressed never putting weight on one's partner. While Michael and I danced, the trainer periodically instructed us to drop our arms to our sides. We continued to follow our choreographed routine but without the benefit of touching each other, which immediately revealed whether each of us was balanced. And the better we became at dancing solo, either practicing alone or dropping our arms when practicing together, the more effectively we danced as partners.

> *The better you are at dancing solo, the better prepared you'll be for dancing with a partner.*

Important parallels exist between being alone on the dance floor and being alone in life. In the following three chapters I'll address various aspects of individual responsibility as they play out in primary relationships, and Chapter 11 will take up the difficult subject of being forced into solitude because of the loss of a loved one. In this chapter, however, I'd like to focus on the type of solo dancing commonly known as being single. Slightly more than half of all Americans between the ages of 20 and 40 now live alone or without an adult partner. That surely represents a major social transformation. And if, as I believe, we are social creatures, and therefore defined mostly by our relationships, it also represents a potential dilemma—if not for everyone who's single, certainly for most of them at least part of the time.

I used the term *potential dilemma* deliberately. Being single doesn't necessarily mean being without significant primary relationships. Yet *being without* continues to be the most common way society defines "being single." And the thing that's presumed missing is always a spouse or some other form of life partner. To be sure, attitudes toward marriage have changed immensely since, say, the 1950s, when the ideal family was embodied in television programs like *Father Knows Best*. The sheer number of single adults and adults in serial, nonexclusive, and other nontraditional relationships attests to that. But in some quarters a certain stigma still attaches to living alone. And, unfortunately, despite the considerable gains they've made in recent decades, women are still more likely than men to be seen as deficient or incomplete if they remain single.

Addressing the social and cultural factors that underpin such wrongheaded attitudes is beyond the reach of this book. But there are steps we can take as individuals to reduce their influence in our own lives and the lives of those we care about. The first step is to acknowledge that we are indeed social animals. We need the company of other human beings in order to grow and be fulfilled. That's why infants raised without enough human contact become emotionally and intellectually stunted. It's also why people placed in solitary confinement for long periods tend to go crazy. Another step you can take, and it's a

> We need the company of other human beings in order to grow and be fulfilled.

corollary of the first, is to admit that living alone can be difficult, usually because the arrangement isn't always, or entirely, voluntary. Very few people actually seek, much less enjoy, complete solitude and by that I mean the absence of all interaction with others. Truth be told, I don't know anyone who wants to live in such an extreme state of separation. This is important to bear in mind because it sheds light on the actual circumstances of the millions of Americans, of all ages, who now live alone.

What I'm suggesting is that the mere fact that more people than ever are living alone doesn't necessarily mean that that's what they truly want to be doing, or at least doing all the time. Indeed, I'd wager that if a poll were taken, many, if not the majority, of these solitaires, as I call them, would say that they'd prefer to have a partner, not necessarily a spouse, but at least a live-in partner. Although our view of the institution of marriage has changed dramatically, our view of romance hasn't. And I'd wager further that almost all of the remaining solitaires, those who honestly don't want or need a live-in partner, would surely say that they do want other kinds of primary relationships. Those might include romantic relationships that don't entail living together, very close friendships, significant family relationships, and/or especially gratifying working collaborations. What all these solitaires have in common, besides their basic living arrangement, is that they don't always get what they want—that is, the kind of companionship they desire, when and how they desire it. Whether it's the 30-something who longs for a partner (live-in or not), the 40-something who's estranged from her siblings, or the 50-something who wishes she had more friends, many solitaires spend more time alone than they really want to. What are these people to do?

Like all major moves in life, solo dancing isn't a problem in and of itself. Widespread solitary living may be a relatively new phenomenon, made possible by certain social and economic shifts in American society, but it's no less natural than living with others. By the same token, as anyone familiar with the history of traditional marriage and nuclear family living knows, shared arrangements aren't necessarily harmonious or healthy. Women, in particular, have suffered under historical conditions that have made them physically and financially dependent on men and therefore forced into marriages that are partially, mostly, or eventually involuntary, and therefore destructive. But with independence and freedom have come new and unique challenges for both men and women. To assume otherwise, to assume that no longer being obliged to get married is a cure for all our relationship ills, is both naïve and self-defeating. To repeat: Living alone can be difficult. That doesn't mean, I hasten to add, that living alone can't be just as fulfilling as sharing your life with someone else. But it does mean that if you're one of the growing number of solitaires, whether by choice or not, you have a great deal of work to do if you wish to do it well. Solo dancing requires just as much practice and persistence as any other type of dance. But if you do

> *Solo dancing can be just as fulfilling as dancing with a partner.*

practice long enough and conscientiously enough, you can shine with gemlike beauty and brightness, just as a diamond solitaire does, all on its own.

One of the challenges single people face is a unique version of the tyranny of perfection, which I introduced in Chapter 5. I've already explored in detail how the inner critic can undermine and even cripple us, if it's allowed to take on a life of its own. Subduing the inner critic so you can concentrate on achieving wholeness rather than chasing perfection is essential to fulfilling yourself as a single person. But the inner critic can be equally destructive in its judgment of others. Indeed, the two often go hand-in-hand: If you permit your inner critic to dominate how you view yourself, you're more likely to permit it to dominate your view of lovers, friends, employees, clients, and so on. When that happens, the people in your life can never measure up and can never please you. In other words, you don't give those you supposedly care about room to stumble, which in effect means that you don't give them room to grow—to practice their own lives, to fill their own life spaces.

> *Solo dancing requires as much practice and persistence as any other kind of dance.*

Among single people who long for a romantic relationship, the inner critic usually gauges others by comparing them to an imaginary ideal that's impossible to match. How that ideal man or woman develops is less important than reducing its power over your behavior. And the most effective way to accomplish that is to turn your attention away from the ideal other, which doesn't exist anyway, to the less-than-ideal you, you as a single person, without a partner. If anything's going to increase your chances of meeting someone with whom you can share the dance of life, it's improving your own dancing skills. Dissatisfied with your relationships? Work on the part of your relationships over which you exercise some degree of control—yourself.

> Increase your chances of finding a partner in the dance of life by becoming the best possible solo dancer.

To borrow the words of Martha Graham, make the role you're playing now, dancing solo, your favorite role, by giving yourself to it wholeheartedly, as if it were the last role you'll ever play.

No doubt you've noticed that I've just described another paradox. In effect, what I said in the last paragraph is that the best way to find a life partner is to give up the search for one. But that's how desire sometimes works. Certain things in life come to us only when we cease striving for them, or at least cease pursuing them directly. This is especially true in situations in which our striving actually is a cover for resistance. Let me clarify what I mean by returning to the dilemma of dancing solo—being a social animal who lives alone. I'm also going to broaden the discussion by including not only the desire for a romantic partner but desire for human companionship of all kinds. No matter how sincere or strong such desires may be, often

> Certain things come to us only when we cease striving for them, especially when our striving is a cover for resistance.

they're distorted by a fear of or discomfort with solitude. Even those who appear to be at ease with their solo lifestyle can be masking an underlying dread.

One of the common ways that the fear and dread manifest themselves is in clutter. The single person fills his days with so many activities, diversions, and other superficialities that he never has to deal with the fact that he's alone, never has to listen to the scary thoughts and feelings that arise when the rest of the world is silent. He's constantly making and answering cell phone calls. He always leaves the television on. He brings his work home every night, turning his personal space into an extension of his office. Maybe some of this stuff actually matters. Maybe some of it's necessary. A lot of it, perhaps most of it, isn't. That's what I mean by clutter: Time-consuming, energy-draining distractions that ultimately are inconsequential. And single people aren't the only ones who fill the emptiness in their lives with such junk, who avoid the lonesome silence by manufacturing comforting noise. Coming to terms with solitude is a task all of us face, which is why what I'm saying here applies to everyone to one degree or another. Some of us sidestep the issue by marrying young, having children, and so on, postponing the difficult solo work until later, when those we love depart or die or otherwise leave us on our own for the first time. In this sense, single people actually have an advantage, because their basic living arrangement gives them the chance to confront a universal problem early in life.

Making peace with your own solitude is important not only

Making peace with solitude is a task all of us face.

because solitude is unavoidable but because developing healthy, fulfilling relationships depends upon it. Those whose attachments to others are tainted by a dread of solitude are out of balance. And because of that, their behavior is likely to be out of sync or out of proportion to circumstance. In particular, they tend to cling excessively, to be possessive, if not domineering, or to panic whenever they're left alone. In some instances, the fear of being left alone, being abandoned, actually outweighs whatever affection the person might feel for her spouse, lover, friend, etc. These relationships are doomed to disappoint if not seriously damage both parties. And even in situations that aren't this extreme, fear masquerading as love is more common than you might think.

So if it happens that at this time you are single, make the most of it, because it's the best gift you can give to any relationships you might enjoy in the future. It's also the best gift you can give to yourself, whatever the future may bring. Take the opportunity to do what everyone must do eventually anyway. What you'll discover when you stop resisting dancing solo, when you surrender yourself to your current role, is that your life will open up. New prospects will present themselves. You will grow in ways you never dreamed imaginable. The very same principles that apply when taking any first steps also do so in this situation: *Give yourself permission to begin again—and again. Liberate yourself from fear by admitting that you're fearful. Take stumbling in stride. Don't let a little pain or discomfort slow you down.* One of the most common mistakes we make is to believe that, merely by virtue of having reached adulthood, we know how to be human beings. But being human is a lifelong

> *Being human is a lifelong practice, a never-ending learning process.*

practice. It's a never-ending learning process. Who we are is as much something we create as it is something we inherit, and the creation is never more than a work-in-progress.

As you practice your solo dance, also keep in mind that the dance itself will dictate its own rhythms and its own length. In other words, stop looking to the calendar for guidance regarding when it's right to live alone, share your life with others, and so on. Along with an image of the ideal mate, many of us also carry an image of the ideal time frame for certain relationships, especially romantic ones. But these time frames are artificial, unnecessary, and, worst of all, get in the way of enjoying life as it is. Note that they also are another way of saying that being single is a state of *being without*. If you adopt such an approach to life, you are in effect defining your identity by what doesn't exist instead of what does. On a practical level, you undermine yourself, because you're diverting your attention and energy away from the world in front of you, which is the only starting place that's available to you for moving forward—for taking steps to fulfillment.

> *During solo dancing, the dance itself will dictate its own rhythms, its own length. Don't accept artificial time frames.*

People who submit to artificial time frames find themselves doing things like getting married simply for the sake of being married, which is almost always disastrous. Even if they don't go that far, their attempts at developing new relationships are usually marred by desperation and desperation is a highly unappealing quality. The harder they try to attract attention, the less attractive they actually become. At one time or another, most of us have experienced being at least a little desperate, when out of loneliness we try to attach ourselves to whomever happens to comes along. And the result is usually the same: Afterward, we feel even lonelier. Searching for the right partner does little more than postpone our date with solitude, the solo dance we must embrace in order to transform the dance into something else. While chasing our ideal mate within our ideal time frame, we're ignoring real opportunities for living fully. If single people risk missing anything of importance, it's that—the life they've been given.

> While you search in vain for your ideal mate within your ideal time frame, you're missing real opportunities for fulfillment.

Before I outline some of the characteristics of a fully realized single life, I must acknowledge a deadline that cannot be ignored, especially by women. And I have in mind, of course, the biological limit to child-bearing. One of the consequences of the decades-long shift in marriage practice in the United States and other industrialized countries is that more and more single women are approaching this limit. And most of them still want to have babies. Whether they will do so and how they will do so are, of course, personal questions that each woman must answer for herself. I wouldn't presume to cast judgment on single motherhood as a life choice. In the years immediately preceding my getting married (which didn't happen, by the way, until I turned 39) I seriously considered giving birth to and raising a child on my own. But I do believe there are ways of going about being a single parent (and now I'm including never-married single fathers as well as divorced parents of both sexes) that are more likely than others to benefit children.

Apart from such practical concerns as having adequate financial resources, the greatest danger single parents face today is isolation. There was a time, not so long ago, when extended families lived under one roof. In addition to a mother and father, children grew up in the company of sisters and brothers, maybe an aunt, uncle, or older cousin, and often grandparents. All of the adults in the household helped in some way with the task of raising kids. But as the basic family unit has grown smaller and less diverse, children are less likely to interact in meaningful ways with adults. And such interaction is necessary to developing a well-rounded personality, reaching maturity, and becoming independent, as well as learning how best to achieve fulfillment. It's the responsibility of the single parent, then, to make sure being single doesn't mean being isolated. Or, to use dance terms: Even when you're dancing solo, choose a dance floor where lots of others are dancing as well. Welcome people of all kinds—men and women, other singles, couples, and so on—into the life you share with your child or children. When possible, invite other adults to mentor your child in whatever special skills they might possess. By doing so, you will also teach your child by example that being

> *When you're dancing solo, choose a dance floor where lots of other people are dancing as well.*

single needn't be a state of impoverishment, that dancing solo can be just as rich and rewarding as any other way of dancing through life.

The problem of isolation isn't restricted to single parents, of course. Quite the contrary. What I've just said applies equally to all solo dancers. Remember, we are our relationships. That's as true of single people as it is of anyone else. Once you cease resisting the solo dance, then discard the artificially imposed images of the perfect mate and proper time frame for this or that life change, you can redirect your attention toward developing a range of other kinds of relationships. And even in this instance, you'll have much better luck if you don't strive for particular kinds of relationships as such but instead engage in particular activities that will in turn bring you into contact with others. Pursue satisfying interests rather than people, and people eventually will show up. What's more, the people who do show up will be people who like you for who you are, because you've so clearly and forcefully embodied your desires. You've taken a stand. What I wrote at the end of Chapter 4 bears repeating: *Nothing will make you more interesting as a person than being interested in the world around you. Those who are passionate about life are the most likely to arouse passion in others.*

> *Those who are passionate about life are the most likely to arouse passion in others.*

Single people who are living fully are comfortable in their own skin. They're centered. They exude confidence. They're fun to be around, largely because they're always looking for

> *Give yourself
> to the role you're
> playing now.
> Dance as if there's
> no tomorrow.*

ways to make life richer, more enjoyable. Since they're not desperate for companionship, they don't scare others away. They're not *on the make*. In other words, they don't convey to strangers that they want something, that they're going to take something away from them, but instead that they have something worthwhile to give. They understand that the key to fulfillment is generosity. This is another way of stating what I said earlier about committing yourself to the role life has assigned to you at this very moment: If you're dancing solo, do it as well as possible. Dance as if there's no tomorrow. Because, truth be told, there may not be. With that possibility in mind, ask yourself this: Does what you're doing now really matter to you? Are you filling your time with clutter because you're afraid of being alone or are you finding ways to *fulfill yourself* in the time you have left because you've given yourself to dancing solo?

Single or not, you should consider routinely setting aside time for literally dancing solo—alone, in your house, in the street, in a field, wherever and whenever the spirit moves you. I do it at home. When no one else is around. And I usually do it during periods of intense emotion. When I'm grieving I dance. When I'm celebrating I dance. Every dance is different. I improvise from one situation to another, allowing the energy of the moment to flow

> *The key to
> fulfillment as a
> solo dancer is
> generosity.*

through me. Try it. Don't concern yourself with doing it perfectly. Instead, *do it completely*, until you've expressed all you have to express, given all you have to give. Whether you're sad or happy, there's nothing more liberating—and life-affirming—than dancing with utter abandon.

EIGHT

Duets

Dancing is love's proper exercise.

—SHAKESPEARE

Choose your partners. If you haven't heard that line in person, you've probably heard it spoken in a movie or television program, maybe just before a square dance is about to start. It's an invitation to men and women to find someone with whom they're willing to form a team, to move in concert across the dance floor. But the couple needn't remain a couple any longer than the duration of a single song. And in some dances—certain traditional folk dances, for instance—the pivotal movement actually involves exchanging partners, spinning from one person to the next, coupling and recoupling as the number progresses. No man and woman stay together for more than a few seconds and sometimes less than that.

On the dance floor of life, by contrast, most of us seek partnerships that endure as long as possible—or "until death do us part." Another important difference is that we tend to view coupling as something that happens *to us*, not something we make happen. We don't so much choose our partners as they choose us. Indeed, that's the widely accepted definition of romantic love—an irresistible, magnetic-like urge to be with another human being, an overwhelming attraction that sweeps us away involuntarily, just as a fast-flowing river might. We *fall* in love, meaning that we fall under someone else's spell, all along hoping that the object of our affection is experiencing the same sense of exquisite helplessness. And if so, maybe we've found our match, the person who'll be our dance partner for life.

What everyone who's fallen in love eventually discovers, of course, is that for romance to last, a couple must have more going for it than romance; and if it's to last a lifetime, much more. This is largely why we participate in the ritual of marriage—to exchange vows of unconditional commitment, a mutual promise that the parties will stay together no matter what, even if at times the relationship is anything but romantic. Most people who get married understand this, at least in principle. But it's almost impossible to appreciate what it will mean in practice, when the proverbial honeymoon is over, the ever-optimistic first phase of love has run its course, and the tedium and trials of day-to-day existence set in. The challenges couples encounter at this point differ greatly, but surmounting the challenges always requires the same response—a reaffirmation of wedding vows.

> *For romance to last, you need much more than romance.*

Usually this happens automatically, without much or any reflection. But during especially difficult periods, the reaffirmation often becomes conscious. A person is pushed to the brink of despair, maybe even imagining leaving or taking the first steps in that direction. Then, more keenly aware than ever of the probable risks and possible rewards, she or he decides to recommit to the marriage. Occasionally, couples even go so far as to reenact their wedding, in what amounts to a fully informed decision. And, ironically, that can be all the more romantic because it represents a love that's no longer naive.

Besides offering hope that romance can in fact last, couples who stay together for life, and *remain in love* while doing so, have much to teach us about the importance of choice in all of our primary relationships, whether they involve spouses, relatives, friends, or coworkers. Generally speaking, the less a relationship is based on choice, the more potential there is for some type of harm being done. Another way to say this is that in a healthy but dependent relationship, the one who has appreciably more power—parent, teacher, supervisor—also bears more responsibility. In Chapter 2, I dealt briefly with the problems that arise when adults abuse their superior

> *The less a relationship is based on choice, the more potential there is for harm being done.*

position to instill in children a self-destructive fear of disapproval and punishment for the harmless stumbling that accompanies normal growth. And in Chapter 10, I'll address in greater detail the same issues as they pertain to relationships in which by design one person possesses more power than the other. The relationship that concerns us here, however, is one in which the preferred condition is an equal division of power—marriage, or some other form of long-term romantic partnership.

Though it might not be obvious, in such partnerships choice entails more than being willing to weather the bad times without giving up on our partners. Because *we are our relationships*, and because the romantic partnership is the most intense and intimate of all relationships, our well-being is inseparable from that of our partners to a degree that we'll never experience in any other relationship of equals. This means that whether we'll continue to grow depends greatly on our partners also continuing to grow, or at least attempting to do so. Or, stated positively: If we hope to fulfill ourselves, we should help create and cultivate romantic relationships that enable our partners to fulfill themselves as well—to fill up

> *Cultivate romantic relationships in which both partners achieve fulfillment— separately and together.*

their life space. This requires going way beyond merely choosing to live with someone else, then passively enduring whatever troubles may come your way. It asks that you actively give yourself to another human being—give your time, your attention, your heart.

Earlier I spoke of achieving grace by surrendering yourself to a new experience. If you stop pretending that you're

> *Generosity
> is the most
> powerful force
> in the universe.*

in control, stop letting fear of missteps and embarrassment keep you trapped on the sidelines of life, in time you'll grow more comfortable, lighter of being, gradually gaining enough mastery to flow smoothly from one moment to the next. Grace, in short, is reached by means of generosity. In a romantic partnership, it's attained through countless small acts of generosity—giving yourself to the relationship again and again and again.

Virtually all romantic relationships begin in a state of excitement. That's stating the obvious, I must confess. In a sense, of course, romance is the very embodiment of excitement, exhilaration, even, for some, ecstasy. What's not always appreciated is that among the many things that romance excites is the imagination. Love may be blind, to be sure, but just as often it's a dream—a dream that intoxicates the dreamer. Much of the pleasure of romance comes from the fantasies that another person

> *Start where
> you are.*

arouses in us. We experience a sense of limitless possibility. Suddenly the horizon expands and everything we could want from another human being seems within reach. All of this is desirable, but only if it's accompanied by *a commitment to starting where we are*. Without that, we run the risk of falling in love with what might be instead of what is. We marry the potential—the person our partner could possibly be—rather than the actual person he or she is. And that, in turn, can lead to bitter disillusionment and/or increasingly disastrous attempts to remake our partners so that he or she better resembles our fantasies.

I want to be clear about this. When you give yourself to another human being, you're essentially saying that you're willing to be affected, influenced, even altered in significant ways by that person. Romantic love simply cannot survive for long in the absence of that kind of openness, and the best partnerships, romantic or otherwise, take us to places we wouldn't or couldn't have gone on our own. But being open to the changes that are inevitable as a romantic partnership evolves is very different from deliberately setting about to fix what you perceive as flaws in your partner. This is a common mistake, so common that perhaps all marriage vows should include an explicit pledge to take the other as he or she is, right here, today, unconditionally. Even then, it may be difficult to keep yourself in check, to avoid becoming a source of *negative* commentary on your mate's behavior, appearance, or mannerisms. My advice? Devote some time to examining what's going on inside you during those moments when he or she bothers you. Take it a step further by imagining that when you're criticizing your partner, you're actually talking to the person who stares back at you in the mirror. You'll be surprised how often your dissatisfaction with others reflects dissatisfaction with yourself.

> *Sometimes dissatisfaction with others reflects dissatisfaction with oneself.*

If that exercise doesn't shed light on the situation, it still helps to remind yourself that the most fruitful way to move from where you are now to somewhere else isn't by offering discouragement but instead a continual supply of encouragement. Don't focus on what your partner isn't doing. That wastes your energy and, worse still, runs the risk of disabling your partner, by making her feel like a failure, which can quickly turn into something uglier— resentment. How often have we unintentionally found ourselves in that situation, only to explain feebly, "All I wanted to do was help." But you can be sure that if you've caused your partner to feel resentment, you haven't helped anyone's cause, including your own. Even if what concerns you is unmistakably a self-destructive habit—a partner giving in to unfounded but paralyzing fear, for example, or drinking excessively—outright disapproval rarely accomplishes anything. Better to appeal to your partner's higher aspirations, rewarding even the smallest improvement with praise, affection, positive attention. Everyone, remember, needs approval. And nothing is more nourishing to the human spirit than receiving the approval of those we care about most, which usually means our spouses and families. Always look for the gold in people. It's there, believe me. And like sunlight on seedlings, paying attention to it, praising it, helps it grow.

Nothing is more nourishing to the human spirit than the approval of those we care about most.

Starting where you are on the dance floor of life also means recognizing that everyone moves at a different pace and follows a different rhythm. In a romantic partnership, timing is everything. Sometimes this is difficult to appreciate because it seems to contradict the defining experience of romance, at least at the outset—a sense of unity, harmony, merging with another human being. Having at long last found your soul mate, your relationship should flow smoothly, right? If it were only that simple. Remember: To keep a roman-tic partnership alive and growing, you and your partner will require much more than romance. For starters, you need to be willing to try again, and again, and yet again, on those days or

> ⟶
> *Look for the gold in people, then help it grow.*

nights together that don't flow smoothly. Everything I've said about taking small steps, overcoming your fear of stumbling, ig-noring the internal critic, and so on applies as well to relation-ships. If you were running a business and experienced a bad week—which every business does—you wouldn't react by shutting the doors, would you? Why then is walking away even an option at the first sign of trouble in the most important of your relation-ships? You can't quit something you haven't really given a chance to succeed. Couples trip; they become confused and

> ⟶
> *From time to time, all couples will find themselves out of sync.*

lost; *they get out of sync,* just as individuals do.

The difference, of course, is that in addition to your own anxieties, self-doubt, and various bad habits, you're now also contending with another person's anxieties, self-doubt, and bad habits, some or many of which you won't even be aware of, since you're still getting to know your partner. And that in turn complicates matters, particularly the issue of control. Besides learning to trust yourself, which is difficult enough, you must learn to trust someone else. The process can't begin until you

acknowledge that the situation, no matter how comfortable or welcoming it
might feel at first, is basically new, unfamiliar, and that to have any hope of gaining some degree of mastery you have to

*Surrender
to romance.*

begin by letting go, by admitting that you aren't in complete
control. Indeed, this is the true meaning of the phrase I used
earlier—surrender to the dance. It's essential that you surrender to the romantic partnership, placing your faith in it despite
not knowing what lies ahead, *despite being at the mercy of forces
that are larger than you.*

The last idea is so important that it needs to be underlined:
One way to read this book is as a guide to dealing with forces
and factors that are larger than you, with special attention
given to certain fundamental situations we all share—romance,
friendship, parenthood, and so on. This overarching relationship, this never-ending dance with what's unknown and beyond our control, is the most important relationship any of us
will ever know. It is the very *dance of life* itself. And at no time
is the dance of life more challenging than when we lose what
we love most, especially spouses, children, and family members, a subject I'll take up in Chapter 11. The reason I'm em-
phasizing the point here is that it leads to a distinction that
couples must appreciate if they want to be fulfilled, both together and separately.

Notice that I say *surrender to the dance* rather than surrender
to your dance partner, and that I then recast the principle as *surrender to romance* instead of surrender to your romantic partner.
This shifts our focus from the individual to the relationship,

where it belongs, not because individuals are less important than their relationships but because whatever contributes to the well-being and longevity of their relationships also best serves their needs as individuals. I don't mean to suggest that the only way to be fulfilled is to form a lifelong romantic partnership. Not in the least, especially these days, when people enjoy more freedom than ever in how they arrange their personal lives. But just about everyone needs and wants lasting relationships of one sort or another. What do you almost always find when you look closely at those who live alone for long periods of time and also achieve fulfillment? Enduring, powerfully nurturing friendships, strong ties to family members, and/or significant associations with individuals or groups who share their interests and values, occupational passions, or favorite pastimes. And in all these instances, the well-being of the individual depends to a great degree on the overall well-being of the relationship. By concentrating on making your relationships robust and fruitful you create the most favorable conditions for maintaining your own psychological health.

One of the immediate benefits of focusing on the relationship is that it helps us avoid the many elements of the *competitive dynamic* that so often destroys romance: accusation (I find fault with you), humiliation (you experience shame), resentment (you get angry, which makes me defensive and angry), and estrangement (we grow apart). Except in extreme cases, when we've chosen or can't escape people who are hopelessly destructive or self-destructive, everything we do with our romantic partners should be based instead on a *cooperative dynamic*—on the assumption that "we're in this together." This

126

> Cooperation and
> continual renewal
> are necessary for
> romance to last.

isn't as easy as it sounds, I admit, even though it's what we tell ourselves repeatedly, most notably when we utter those much-touted marriage vows. Sometimes it takes a long time, even years, to put our vows into practice, to be able to embody our verbal commitment to togetherness in our everyday actions. Truly giving yourself to a romantic partnership, placing your faith in it despite the ups and downs, the trials and disappointments, is not something that happens overnight. Indeed, it's not something that's ever finished, completed. The kind of deep, mature, fruitful love that I have in mind here is always a *work in progress*, something that needs to be reaffirmed and renewed repeatedly. Without continual renewal the partnership may last, though that's doubtful, but the romance surely won't.

How can you tell when two individuals are cooperating in order to achieve a common good rather than competing so that one or the other can gain dominance? When any and all problems that come up are viewed as *our problems*. It would be foolish, of course, to ignore the fact that one or the other party to a romance may be more or less culpable for this or that particular difficulty. Often one person is right, or

> Love is
> always a work
> in progress.

righter, the other wrong, maybe very wrong. But it's even more foolish to assume that such difficulties can be resolved outside the context of the relationship, through the efforts of only one of the individuals acting in isolation. Stated in practical terms, assigning blame for a problem, which creates distance between people, is less effective than offering to help resolve it, which tends to bring people together.

The difference I'm highlighting here may seem slight but it's essential to understanding how romantic partnerships endure. When you've truly given yourself to an intimate relationship, your greatest concern isn't being right, isn't being the one who comes out on top, but instead keeping the relationship alive and healthy and growing. That entails two kinds of responsibility: (1) owning up to *your own* fears, weaknesses, and bad habits, and (2) always conveying to your partner that you believe in him or her despite *your partner's* fears, weaknesses, and bad habits. This is why therapists recommend that when couples discuss problems they describe their own feelings (*your anger confuses me*) rather than attack the character of the other person (*you're a heartless person*). It's also why they're adamant that couples focus such discussions on behavior while simultaneously expressing loyalty to the partnership (*you're a wonderful guy, and I'm crazy about you, but when you yell at me I get scared and sad*). Instead of throwing stones, show that you're willing to help carry the weight.

> *Instead of throwing stones, help carry the weight.*

This approach won't always yield positive results. Nor does getting positive results in one instance guarantee that it'll work in another. Inevitably there will be times when you and your partner are at cross purposes, moving in different, even opposite directions, or at different speeds. Everything will seem like a struggle. You'll bump into each other. You may even lose contact with each other or begin to seem like strangers. No matter how hard you try, you won't be able to dance together. This is to be expected in long-term relationships. In the heat of the moment, in particular, it may be impossible to see, feel, or think about anything but the heat. A time-out may then be needed to allow each person to cool down, put things back in perspective, and, most important, reaffirm the underlying commitment to the relationship.

You also have to be careful not to confuse taking responsibility for the well-being of the partnership with taking responsibility for the behavior of your partner, which may seem like a loving gesture but actually undermines your partner and ultimately the partnership itself. This mistake is so common and so potentially damaging that it needs to be described in more detail. Let's begin by exposing the assumption that underpins the mistake, an assumption that's rarely questioned: That having reached adulthood, we automatically know how to love other people. Is this what you assume? It's certainly what *I* assumed, and for a long time after I graduated from childhood. Truth be told, I didn't give it any

Loving well, like living well, comes only after lots of practice.

thought until what I had thoughtlessly taken for granted had repeatedly brought me to grief. Only after enduring several baffling and disappointing romantic relationships did it dawn on me that my type of love might be naïve, misguided, and sometimes self-destructive. That's when I came to the sobering realization that proper love, *mature* love, requires practice, a lifetime of practice—that there's a second, highly significant sense in which love is a work-in-progress.

Having seen me argue that being human is something that must be learned, maybe it won't surprise you to now see me assert that love has to be learned, too. Among the many aspects of the practice of love is developing the ability to distinguish between caring that celebrates and nurtures independence and caring that does precisely the opposite, rendering those we supposedly love more dependent, weaker, and less aware. Such misplaced "care" can assume many forms, but it almost always leads to denial and deception, whereby you find yourself routinely making excuses for your partner's bad behavior, even going to great lengths to prevent others from finding out about it. Addiction, physical and mental abuse, habitual anger, habitual fear, wastefulness, laziness, infidelity: the list of behaviors that we cover up or cloak in silence is endless. If you're familiar with twelve-step programs, then you know the term that's commonly used for this situation—enabling. By denying or masking the destructive behavior of your partner, you actually become a co-conspirator. You enable your partner to continue indulging in his or her bad habits.

In a strong partnership, each person is capable of standing on his or her own two feet.

On the dance floor of life, as on the dance floor itself, the strongest and most smooth-flowing couples, the couples that are most likely to stay together for the duration of the dance, are those in which both individuals are capable of standing on their own two feet.

> *Encouraging independence should be a long-term goal in relationships between equals.*

Combine this principle with the other main principle of this chapter—surrender to the dance of love—and you create a comprehensive vision that will guide you and your partner through most of life's challenges. This is an ideal, of course, a state of being that we should always strive toward but will never fully or permanently realize. That said, trying to put into practice a vision that stresses both the well-being of the partnership and the personal responsibility of each partner gives the couple the means to make common cause when everything else seems to be in contention, to find true north during times of disorientation.

In effect, this twofold vision serves as the overarching long-term goal by which all short-term goals can be judged. Should I lean on my partner for support? Maybe, if it doesn't go on too long, leading to unhealthy clinging or crippling dependency. Should I allow my partner to lean on me? Yes, certainly, but not if it cripples me, exhausts me, and only so long as my partner

> *Mutual generosity is a continual exchange of energy that nurtures each partner while strengthening the partnership itself.*

is actively engaged in regaining her strength, her poise, her ability to stand on her own without being propped up. This is how *mutual generosity* operates on a day-to-day basis. It's a continual exchange of energy that not only nurtures each individual but also strengthens the overall partnership. Later, when I take up the subject of healthy dependent relationships (parent-child, teacher-student, and the like), I'll attempt to demonstrate why the most important long-term goal of such relationships should be to help dependents to become independent. But encouraging independence also should be a primary long-term goal of equal relationships because, of course, a great number of adults haven't yet learned to stand on their own two feet.

Which brings me back to the issue of control. Before I go any further, though, let me address those readers—and surely there are some—who are wondering why I make so much of control. Of all the areas of difficulty a couple may face, including communication, money, physical intimacy, parenting, socializing with others, and so on, the one that's most often overlooked is power, which is why, by the way, the destructive role of humiliation also is insufficiently appreciated. In any exchange between human beings, identity is either being affirmed or denied, nurtured or eroded. And the integrity of identity depends on possessing at least some measure of control over one's circumstances. We are, after all, human first, no matter how completely we *identify* with our roles as spouse, parent, friend, neighbor, coworker, citizen. Generosity cannot be mutual unless this fundamental fact is recognized and respected. I've already discussed how the paradox of needing a sense of control while letting go at the right times operates in the case of the individual. For romantic partners, it entails a never-ending process of give-and-take during which one person leads, then the other, the roles constantly switching back and forth as the couple travels together through life.

Modern interpretive dancers sometimes warm up by performing an exercise called contact improvisation. The rules are simple and the potential results quite illuminating. Participants divide into pairs. Each pair is allowed to move any way they wish as long as their bodies are always touching. Here's what makes it fun: The point of contact can be as slight as a fingertip, unfamiliar as an elbow touching a knee, or as forceful as a full embrace, but the couple must never cease moving, which means that the contact point also continually changes. I encourage you to try this exercise with your romantic partner. It'll seem awkward at first but if you place your trust in the relationship, if you give yourself to the energy that's moving between you and your partner, you'll discover at least three things. On the one hand, even though you're dancing with someone else, you enjoy a surprising amount of freedom to twist and turn and otherwise improvise. You can also skip across the room, slide along the floor, occupy the space any way you like. On the other hand, you must always be mindful of your partner's movements so as not to lose contact with him or her. What's more, if indeed your partnership is one of equals, two characteristics are required of each partner—an *ability* to lead and a *willingness* to follow—if the dance is to last.

> *Each partner in a romantic relationship must possess both the ability to lead and a willingness to follow.*

The same is true on the dance floor of life. By establishing a rhythm between leading and following, couples can maximize individual expression while keeping their relationship alive and healthy. The form that this give-and-take process assumes will vary drastically from one couple to the next, depending on circumstance; differences in taste, interest, and personality; factors outside the relationship that require attention or exercise influence; and so on. I might be especially enthused about an upcoming trip, for example, so I take the lead in making preparations, whereas you become inspired during the trip, directing us toward unexpected pleasures. Or perhaps today I yield to your desire to attend a football game, an enthusiasm I don't necessarily share, and tomorrow you accompany me to a concert that doesn't exactly make your heart beat faster. Sometimes being committed to the give-and-take of a romantic relationship means allowing each other to go our separate ways. But whatever shape such acts of mutual generosity may take, they are the most promising way to perform "love's proper exercise," when each person is standing on his or her own two feet, doing his or her part, while choosing at every turn to continue *moving in concert*.

NINE

The Dance of Life

Tonight, I'll take you to the Mardi Gras
Where we will dance and sing.

—IRVING BERLIN

Ballroom dances are divided into different categories based on the patterns they describe on the dance floor. The first of the two major groups includes the rumba, cha cha, mambo, salsa, and swing, which are known collectively as spot dances because each couple remains in roughly the same place as the dance progresses. As long as the partners have enough room, their movements are independent of the movements of other couples around them. A man and woman performing a spot dance are so focused on each other that they could just as well be the only couple on the dance floor. Indeed, the intense intimacy of the salsa, swing, and so on may be what the playwright George Bernard Shaw had in mind when he quipped, "Dancing is the vertical expression of a horizontal desire."

So it is off the dance floor, as well. Every couple needs time apart from the rest of the world—to create a sturdy, clearly defined partnership; to address potentially disruptive differences and strengthen ties; to protect the relationship from external threats and wasteful distractions; and, yes, to give expression to their most intimate desires. Couples need a place of their own, a separate physical and emotional space where they can *practice* being a couple, finding the basic moves and rhythms that best serve their needs as well as experimenting with different ways of putting the principle of mutual generosity into prac-

> *Couples
> need time apart
> from the world to
> practice being
> a couple.*

tice. By making room for the psychological equivalent of spot dancing, couples increase the likelihood of achieving wholeness and therefore becoming more balanced, which is just as essential to partnerships as it is to individuals. What I have in mind here is the idea of centering, specifically, centering as a requirement for balanced movement or, using terms more suitable for the dance of life, handling change in a more graceful manner. And who doesn't want that?

One of the primary lessons I learned as a Fred Astaire dance instructor is that students who are centered are easier to train than those who aren't. "Centered" is a slippery term, of course, one that's both overused and often underdefined, a combination sure to cause confusion. As far as the individual dancer is concerned, centering as I'm employing the word means being of one mind about and fully engaged with the task at hand. It's not that a well-centered person won't stumble when attempting something new. Missteps are inevitable for everyone. But people who are centered, both off and on the dance floor, tend not to squander energy on fear of failure (fixating on the future) or embarrassment for having failed (fixating on the past). They aren't so burdened by guilt or regret, so beside themselves with anger, jealousy, or obsession, that their concentration is scattered or drifts away from the here-and-now. Imperfection, as I said earlier, isn't an impediment to fulfillment but being a slave to these other destructive impulses certainly is—*because it diverts or depletes the energy you need for the activity at hand*.

> *Anything that diverts or depletes energy prevents fulfillment.*

For couples, being centered means all of the foregoing plus not being consumed by a desire to dominate or possess the other person. Centered couples may not always move gracefully through life but they know that the key to doing so is discovering—through persistence and practice—just the right interplay of give and take, surrender and control, that best suits their abilities, needs, and personalities. Even on the dance floor, where traditionally men lead and women follow, the man doesn't actually control the woman, nor does the woman really submit to the man. They aren't, after all, participating in a wrestling match but instead a harmonious union of bodies in motion. What's more, if both dancers play their assigned roles conscientiously, the man's movements will call attention to those of his partner. We urge our male students to think of themselves as the frame, so that everyone's eyes will be drawn to the picture—their female partners. When both the man and the woman are playing their respective parts in a particular dance, a *creative tension* develops between

> *In a healthy couple, the give and take of energy produces creative tension.*

them. They push back against each other ever so gently but consistently while never losing their own composure—also, of course, while continually moving. When a couple is dancing properly, both partners feel this tension in their hands and arms at the same time. This is centering in action and, most important, it energizes the couple.

Away from the dance floor, where the vitality and longevity of the romantic partnership depends on partners continually trading the lead, being centered entails similar elements: just enough tension to keep energy flowing back and forth but never at the cost of either partner's balance. Each partner both gives and takes energy while always striving to keep the energy flowing. Timing, it must be remembered, is everything. And mastering timing requires practice, lots and lots of practice. Everything in life is rhythmical, in ebbs and flows, and is subject to seasonal change. Every individual has his or her own rhythm. So does every couple. And so do larger groups—families, networks of friends and coworkers, communities, and whole societies. That's what I'd

> *To learn timing requires practice and persistence and still more practice.*

like to address now, the various social contexts that serve as fields of play for our primary relationships. The dance of life doesn't take place in a vacuum. Despite appearances, we're never really alone on the dance floor, which means that our emotional and behavioral repertoire must include more than spot dances if we're going to be fulfilled either as individuals or couples.

*L*et's return to the first stage of romance, when hearts open wide and the horizon suddenly seems limitless. At that seemingly miraculous moment, we're certain we've met our life-long mate, certain in large part because the object of our affection seems capable of meeting our every need. He or she is the very personification of promise. What a joy that is, also a relief, especially if you've been lonesome for a long time or previous relationships have been disappointing. But beware: No single human being can satisfy all your relationship needs. Allow yourself the delicious but temporary pleasure of being made to feel that way, but don't allow yourself to believe it because it almost always leads to heartache by setting up unrealistic expectations in you while placing an unfair burden on your partner. It also tends to stifle individual growth by discouraging, even at times punishing, the development of other enriching relationships.

No one person can satisfy all your relationship needs.

In earlier times, couples were less likely to make this mistake because they lived with or very near extended families and enjoyed closer ties to neighbors and friends. Today, by contrast, couples, as well as individuals, tend to think of themselves in terms of smaller and smaller social units, not really needing steady, meaningful contact with a range of other people. This is another one of those paradoxical situations in which the only way to grow is by letting go. Abandon the idea that your primary relationship is an island unto itself, mostly self-sufficient and independent of the world, and you'll strengthen the relationship. Why? Because no matter what you may believe, your primary relationship does in fact exist within and depend upon a web of other relationships. What's more, that web of secondary relationships is a constant source of new energy, which stimulates and feeds the primary relationship, keeping it from becoming stagnant. It also provides opportunities for individual fulfillment that may be insufficient or entirely absent in the primary relationship. Nothing could be more naive than to think that all of your interests, desires, and preoccupations will coincide with those of your partner, or that sharing every imaginable activity is the key to well-being and lasting love. Yes, a certain amount of overlap is desirable, though how much is surprisingly variable. Some couples flourish as much as they do precisely because they spend a lot of time apart, engaged in different pursuits. Others prefer the opposite, occasionally going so far as to work and live together.

The only way to grow is by letting go.

Most couples fall somewhere between these extremes. And finding the combination that best suits us—the *right balance*—is a matter of experimentation. In other words, practice. You're probably tired of hearing that word. And no one could blame you. But I'm repeating it for good reason: I want to underscore the value of persistence, trying again and again, being willing to risk stumbling in order to gain a degree of mastery. Beyond that, I want to stress action—that as important as solitary contemplation may be, ultimately we fulfill ourselves through the countless small acts we perform each day. Step by step, moment by moment. Remember the basic principle that I described in Chapter 1, that (*in life*) *grace is to change as* (*in dance*) *balance is to movement?* Later I made explicit an even more fundamental idea—that life *is* change. That's why dance—more specifically, dancing through life—works well as a metaphor for the human condition, especially when it involves couples. Simply stated, dance is relationship in motion. So is life.

> *Like dance,*
> *life is relationship*
> *in motion.*

Another way of putting this is that motion—change—is unavoidable. So the question that each of us faces isn't whether we'll change, or whether things around us will do so, but instead how to deal with change that's sure to come, and come continually, from birth until we draw our final breath. My general answer is that we must first accept the inevitability of change, then devote ourselves to developing ways of relating to change that have some chance of leading to fulfillment. Acceptance requires generosity, giving of oneself. Applied to the social and cultural contexts within which we live and that sustain our existence, this means recognizing that your primary relationship is part of a complex, interdependent web of relationships. Although the dance floor is a much simpler, safer, and more predictable setting than that in which the dance of life occurs, relevant parallels exist in this instance, as well. Besides spot dances, for example, the other major category based on overall pattern is comprised of the so-called moving dances, which include the fox-trot, waltz, tango, and quick-step, among others. These dances, also known as progressive dances, are similar in that they all require couples to move around the dance floor in a circular pattern. And it's customary for the circles, whose size and pace may vary, to turn counterclockwise. To follow this pattern is known as *traveling down the line of dance.*

> *Your primary relationship is always part of a complex, interdependent web of relationships.*

Learning to travel the line of dance is essential to ballroom dancing, and it starts with each couple seeing itself within the context of other couples, all in motion at the same time and within the same space. The aim is to always advance gracefully, never breaking rhythm or colliding with others. If a couple hesitates or stops short, they become an obstacle to other couples. If they reverse direction, traveling against the line of dance, they cause confusion, disruption, possibly throwing some or all of the dance floor off balance. This isn't an argument against personal freedom or for blindly following convention. Think of *always moving* and *always moving in the same direction* as the equivalent of the rules in contact improvisation; they are designed to bring about the maximum amount of individual fulfillment within the context of multiple relationships. In

> *Always travel down the line of dance.*

effect, the rules create a framework for serving two highly desirable goals at the same time. Once you get accustomed to traveling the line of dance, you discover that there are as many ways to do so as there are couples.

Similarly, couples traveling around the dance floor of life must learn how to take advantage of the overall direction in which events are flowing, the basic rhythms and broad currents of life, along with the daily cadence of ups and downs. "To every thing there is a season," the book of Ecclesiates in the Bible says, "and a time to every purpose under heaven." What "season" and "purpose" mean in this context may at first be unclear, but the rest of that Old Testament passage provides clues: birth and death, planting and harvesting, weeping and laughing, gaining and losing, taking apart and putting back together, speaking and keeping silent, and so on. These are universal human experiences, representing some of the basic moves in the dance of life. On the dance floor, obviously, the line of dance is easy to detect because it always flows in the same direction and it's always in plain sight. Not so off the dance floor. More often than not, the way we learn about flow in that realm is by trial and error—testing the boundaries of the possible.

The basic tenets of the Serenity Prayer also apply to couples: Yes, to be sure, there are limits to what we can control and what we can accomplish. That's one of the implications of the concept that *we are our relationships*. It's also simply a fact of life. But sometimes the only way to discover the limits is to take action, take a stand, take steps, then adjust accordingly. More important than getting it right the first time is being alert to resistance and being willing to shift course, not just once but over and over again. We need constant awareness and flexibility, plus the courage to admit we're wrong. We need to view life as a series of course corrections. By adopting this perspective, not only do we give ourselves the best chance of filling our life space, we eventually come to see that the proper attitude toward life as a whole is humility.

Arrogance is based on the erroneous notion that we're in control of things that can't be controlled, that we know things that can't be known, and especially that it's possible to live without making mistakes. Humility, by contrast, assumes that to live fully making missteps is unavoidable. To approach the world with humility means to not assume ahead of time what's possible, what's knowable. Humility comes when we realize that the process of finding those limits never ends. From the standpoint of arrogance, life is to be overpowered, tamed, and subjected to our purposes. From the standpoint of humility, life is to be respected, learned from, and worked with. Our purposes reach fruition only when we align them with the rhythms of life. Arrogance is a form of combat that brings destruction. Humility is a form of dance that brings delight. I've already used the following image but I believe it's worth revisiting because it so clearly conveys the most productive way to think about flow and the line of dance as they apply to the dance of life. Picture a sailboat. The pilot chooses a course, and then trims his sails to take full advantage

> *In life, the only way to stay on course is to be alert to change and, when the time is right, to be willing to change.*

> *Arrogance brings destruction. Humility brings delight.*

of prevailing winds and currents. Most important, whenever the wind or water shifts he alters the sails accordingly. He stays on course, eventually reaching his destination, not by rigidly adhering to a preconceived plan but by always paying attention to the changes taking place in his environment *and* adapting to those changes when circumstances call for it.

Occasionally our worlds become so topsy-turvy, so unpredictable, that it's best to seek cover and wait out the storm before attempting to more forward. Examples might be a spouse or child becoming terminally ill or a family losing its mortgage because the father or mother has lost a job. Other times we get in our own way, sabotaging ourselves (by succumbing to fear, self-doubt, guilt, anger, or other destructive habits). But apart from overly chaotic life situations and personal difficulties that arise within the relationship itself, the challenges reasonably healthy couples usually face on a day-to-day basis are recognizing external resistance and reacting to it in a timely way.

This isn't to say that we should give up the moment we meet resistance. Nothing that a couple might attempt together—purchase and fix up a house, raise a family, run a business—will be free of struggle or setbacks. But this is precisely why the concept of *practice* is so important. You persist, you endure, you

> *You achieve fulfillment by doing, and doing again, and if that doesn't work, doing it a different way.*

achieve fulfillment, by doing, and doing again, and, if that doesn't work, doing it a different way. How long should you persist before you decide that a particular effort isn't working? How many times should you try again before *doing it a different way*? There are no hard and fast guidelines. But as in all life situations, you should be vigilant about succumbing to old bad habits and developing new ones, being thrown off-balance, or continually losing energy without being replenished on a regular basis. These are signs that you're not traveling down the line of dance—that you're drifting away from your particular *lifeline*.

Also keep in mind the difference between long-term and short-term goals, in particular, how short-term goals require constant adjustment. Periodically review your long-term goals to make sure they truly represent your highest aspirations. We sometimes lose our way because we've mistaken a short-term goal for a long-term one. The pragmatic test for telling the difference is as simple as it is revealing: The most fruitful long-term goals always concern character—who you are and what you can become. Consequently, they tend not to change. Fulfillment, or filling your allotted life space as an individual, in your primary relationships and social groups is an excellent example of a long-term goal. Making money, excelling in a particular sport, becoming one of the best in your profession, inventing a new widget, and the like— these should be seen as short-term goals, or perhaps midterm

> *The most fruitful long-term goals concern character— who you are and what you can become.*

goals, and thus subject to change as circumstance dictates. Why? Because they may or may not bring what you ultimately need—fulfillment.

If your eyes are open to what's going on around you, if you've been practicing making adjustments when changes in your environment require it, and if you're not distracted by fear, regret, or other bad habits, you'll know when it's time to adapt. If, however, you then stubbornly maintain your course, you'll expend energy without making any headway. You may start losing ground. And what you resist will persist until you abandon your arrogance, acknowledging that you've reached a limit to what you can control, to what you can comprehend. With that you gain much-needed humility and a renewed respect for the mystery of life, which is wisdom in action.

> *What you resist will persist.*

After encountering resistance again and again, it's sometimes wise to shift social contexts altogether—in effect, transferring from one dance floor to another. To fill up your life space, as I've already pointed out, you must be willing to experiment, to determine through action how much room you may have. But even more fundamental than that is discovering *where* to act, in other words, which of life's countless dance floors is best for you. For reasons both obvious (background, personality, individual circumstance) and elusive, people find it easier to flourish in some contexts than in others. Human beings are social animals, but they're not equally suited to all social situations.

> *Respect is wisdom in action.*

Like birds taking to the air and fish in water, each of us must find his or her own element, the particular set or sets of circumstances in which we are most likely to achieve fulfillment.

This is an extension of an idea I introduced earlier—that to avoid the damaging behavior of others as well as to counter the self-destructive influence of the inner critic, it's crucial that we surround ourselves with nurturing people who appeal to our better instincts and encourage us when we stumble. Since most significant human change and personal development occurs within the context of relationships, our well-being depends to a great extent upon the well-being of the social groups to which we belong.

> *Find your element—the social settings in which you're most likely to flourish.*

But the conditions that make us feel *at home in the world* include much more than the people we might encounter along the way. Some of us revel in physical activities; others prefer mental or cultural pursuits. Big cities disturb certain people while putting others at peace. Just as many people loathe manual labor as love it, and still others prefer work that allows them to serve rather than supervise. Not everyone finds living in the mountains or along a river a source of inspiration. Nor do all of us derive the same degree of satisfaction from involvement in religious, fraternal, or civic affairs. There is, of course, no end to the different ways people can arrange their lives. And it may well be that you've already discovered the dance floors where you do your best. But if you haven't, or if what once interested and energized you no longer does, I urge you to adopt the same playful, pragmatic approach that you would at the start of any new endeavor. If you think you've seen it all, it's likely you're eyesight is failing. If you believe you've exhausted what the dance of life has to offer, you've done nothing more than exhaust your own imagination.

That may sound harsh. I don't mean to imply that it's always possible to switch dance floors, no matter how much we may want to or how clearly we recognize the need for such a shift in circumstances. Few of us are in a position to walk away from our jobs, at least not without the right opportunity and a great deal of preparation. Family responsibilities must be fulfilled and friends and neighbors must be taken care of, no matter how unwanted or unpleasant doing so may be at any particular moment. Sometimes terrible things—like disease or injury, natural disaster, or loss—simply cannot be avoided. Sometimes the only control you can exercise in such situations is whatever control you may have over your own reaction to what's happening. But this is all the more reason to cultivate an attitude of humility. And, as I've been saying all along, I mean *clear-eyed* humility, which combines a deep, abiding respect for life with a willingness to recognize that life isn't necessarily a Mardi Gras. By cultivating humility, you'll be more likely to put whatever comes your way into the proper perspective, which will enable you to continue dancing through life. When things are going well, you won't waste energy on

> *If you think you've exhausted what the dance of life has to offer, you've done nothing more than exhaust your own imagination.*

small stuff—the little pains and minor disappointments—because you know that big stuff is almost certainly coming up. And when the big stuff does arrive, you won't be so surprised that you're paralyzed. You won't be defeated. No matter how hard it gets, you won't cease taking action—you'll

> *Don't waste your energy on the small stuff, because the big stuff is coming.*

continue to be an active agent instead of becoming a passive victim.

Have you ever noticed that what's almost always missing or deficient in those who are defeated or world-weary is *gratitude*? This is no accident. To be sure, life isn't always or even mostly a Mardi Gras. But it's never anything less than a gift—one that we haven't earned and don't deserve. Keeping this in mind at all times will increase the odds that your many labors will bear fruit. This is what I meant by saying that generosity

> *Generosity is gratitude in action.*

is the most powerful force in the universe, because generosity is how gratitude plays out in the world, be it with regard to our romantic partners, families, friends, coworkers, or neighbors. While life as such may be indifferent to individual needs and wants, no approach to life is more potentially fruitful for the individual than generosity, especially generosity of spirit, or magnanimity. By giving your all to the dance of life you give yourself the best chance to achieve fulfillment.

TEN

Taking the Lead

Every day, the whole day
from the minute you get up is
potentially a dance.

—DEBORAH HAY

In addition to romantic coupling, in which partners are equal, there is a second kind of primary
relationship that all of us experience, and need if
we're going to become fully actualized human beings.
Examples include parent/child, teacher/student,
manager/employee, and caregiver/client. In each
instance, the ideal condition is one of dependency.
One partner takes the lead, the other follows. They
aren't equals, nor do we expect or want them to be.
As you may recall, my epiphany regarding relationships didn't occur in the context of romance but instead work (triggered by a profound personal loss,
which I'll say more about in the following chapter).

As a young, inexperienced Fred Astaire manager who was determined to make her studio the best in the country, I was spending most of my waking hours on the job, interacting with staff and students. The studio was my life, which meant that the well-being of the studio was inseparable from my own health, both physically and emotionally. Why then, I asked myself, should I stand for anything less than creative, constructive *work relationships?*

At the same time, I became convinced that financial success also depends on the quality of those relationships, from how I related to my instructors to how they related to their students. First and foremost, I was in a people business. Taking proper care of my employees was simply sound business practice. This was a profound realization for me, leading to a complete transformation not only in how I trained staff and managed studios but also in how I approached all relationships. But it took a great deal of experimentation and observation to appreciate fully how *healthy but dependent* relationships differ from healthy equal ones. The dances performed by a parent and child or teacher and student place special obligations on the person charged with leading. The first obligation is to recognize that there is indeed an element of obligation and, more important, to accept that fact. Taking this first step can be difficult, if not impossible, for some people under certain circumstances. Unlike romantic relationships, which we consider a blessing, dependent relationships sometimes feel like an imposition, an unwelcome and unpleasant duty, if not an outright curse.

> *Everyone needs healthy dependent relationships.*

To be sure, the degree of imposition varies from relationship to relationship and, within any particular relationship, from one day to the next. But those who yearn to be parents, deeply enjoy mentoring or caring for others, or are devoted to their work will nonetheless have occasions when they become exasperated, wanting nothing more than relief from the demands of their relationships. Equal partners, of course, also occasionally wish to escape. The difference is that in dependent relationships the person who leads bears more responsibility, sometimes a great deal more. In the most extreme case, conceiving and raising children, the full weight of responsibility falls on the parents' shoulders, at least during the early years. But even in these situations, choice plays a crucial role. How, you might wonder, could that be true when you're presented with only one option—taking care of those who depend upon you? How can you choose what's going to happen anyway?

> *In dependent relationships, the person who leads bears more responsibility, sometimes a great deal more.*

Yet another paradox, I'm afraid. Part of the answer is that sometimes you won't be able to bring yourself to choose. You'll simply endure whatever hardships have beset you, meeting your obligations as best as possible while hoping that better times lay ahead. You'll remain faithful to long-term goals—say, being a nurturing father and standing by your children until they can stand on their own—despite the short-term setbacks. And if you've been similarly tested before, you'll draw strength from the hard-earned knowledge that precisely this level of commitment is necessary

for relationships to reach fruition. Psychologists call this being able to *delay
gratification,* and they insist that we
can't reach maturity without it. They're
right. Setting only short-term goals,
which can be met easily and quickly, is
indistinguishable from wandering aim-
lessly. Because you lack direction, you greatly reduce your
chances of getting anywhere desirable or worthwhile. But there's
another way to approach the dilemma of dependent relationships, and it starts with viewing responsibility as something larger
and more significant than mere duty.

> *Setting only
> short-term goals
> is the same as
> wandering aimlessly.*

When someone else's well-being, whether by choice or circumstance, is placed in our hands, the normal reaction is
heightened awareness. This isn't something we think about or
decide to do; it just happens. Because we care about or, in
some cases, love the other person, we pay closer attention to
their needs, problems, unique traits, and so on. The more we
know someone, the better equipped we are to help in ways that
best encourage his or her growth. Another way of saying this is
that we become more *responsive* to those who depend upon us.
And responsiveness is the soul of responsibility. In its most
refined form, responsiveness becomes empathy—awareness-
through-identification—and finally compassion. Anyone who
has children knows what I mean. Parents who are really meant
to be parents can't help but identify with their sons and
daughters, experiencing heartache whenever they suffer, elation when they're happy, relief when some trial or disappointment has passed.

> *Responsiveness is the soul of responsibility.*

Cultivating some measure of empathy is also necessary in our relationships with students and apprentices, employees and coworkers, patients, clients, and customers. Responsiveness is the foundation of *right action*, which, in the context of dependent relationships, is action that takes into account both where the other person is now and where they want or need to go to be able to fill their unique life space. In the dance business, I train to impart skills, but I hire on the basis of behavior and character traits. And after I bring someone onboard, I take pains to get further acquainted with who they really are. The better I understand a new employee, the more effectively I can motivate and mentor them. Until you've danced in someone else's shoes, either literally or imaginatively, you can't give them what they really need because you don't know what they need, know from the *inside* what troubles them, what excites them, what might best fulfill their highest aspirations. Your actions will be out of sync with their rhythms and movements. You'll cause confusion, frustration, or worse.

This is where choice comes back into the picture, because the larger sense of responsibility that I've just described applies to all relationships, indeed, to the entire world. Choose to cultivate responsiveness not because you're required to do so in a particular dependent relationship but because being fully present and alive to the world makes you feel more alive, makes your life bigger, richer, more resonant. Responsiveness

> *Responsiveness leads to right action.*

can be much more than a short-term obligation; it's potentially a way of being in the world. When responsiveness is taken to the level of compassion, it's the most worthy of all the long-term character goals you can set for yourself. Every moment of every day, to paraphrase avant-garde choreographer Deborah Hay, is part of the dance of life. And every moment of every day we're given the chance to choose how we'll participate.

No one, of course, is capable of being fully responsive to everything all the time. Life is complex, contradictory, messy, and sometimes just downright baffling. We're subject to our own cadences of engagement and disengagement and follow patterns of concentration that suit our singular needs, interests, and personalities. In addition, different things compete for our attention as each day, week, and month unfolds—all of which means that we have to decide what most deserves our care at any particular moment while remaining nimble enough to shift focus when circumstance calls for it. Remember that relationships always involve energy. In healthy dependent relationships, the person who leads tends to give more energy than she receives. She therefore risks becoming emotionally drained, which in turn means that she must conserve her internal resources, choosing wisely when and where to employ them. If you're exhausted, you'll be of little or no use to anyone.

Nor will you be of use to others if you're numb from overstimulation, paralyzed by fear or doubt, or distracted by

> *In healthy dependent relationships, the person who leads tends to give more energy than she receives.*

ambition, obsession, or some form of addiction. It's impossible to be properly responsive to someone who's dependent upon us without remaining centered and balanced. You can't listen to what others are saying if the voices in your head are too loud and insistent. You can't give yourself to the dance of life if you're consumed by anger, resentment, guilt, jealousy, and the like. By the same token, being fully present and alive to someone else doesn't always, or even often, translate into aggressive action or intervention. To take the lead is not to dominate and possess but to guide and encourage. As parents, mentors, and supervisors, we sometimes lose sight of the overarching aim of *healthy* dependent relationships, which is to create the conditions that lead to *independence*. That's what makes healthy dependent relationships healthy: They're always moving in the direction of ever-greater autonomy. Another way of saying this is that the primary long-term goal of dependent relationships should be to eliminate the need for the relationship, ideally by transforming it into a relationship of equals, although sometimes people simply separate and go their own ways.

> *To take the lead is not to dominate or possess but to guide and encourage.*

The most recognizable examples of relationships whose purpose is to encourage the dependent partner to achieve independence are those between parent and child and teacher and student. Nothing pleases a parent or teacher more than watching their young charges become stronger, better skilled, more confident, needing less and less to be led around the dance floor of life. But the same dynamic is at work whenever a nurse

helps restore a patient to health, a
manager enables an employee to fulfill duties or initiate improvements
without requiring oversight, or a service provider satisfies a customer's
needs. The partner who begins by following, even placing his weight on the
other person, eventually learns how to
stand on his or her own two feet.

> ~~◑~~
> *The long-term
> goal of healthy
> dependent
> relationships
> is to nurture
> independence.*

If independence is the primary long-term goal of the
healthy dependent relationship, then obviously a telltale sign
that such a relationship isn't healthy is when the dependency
is needlessly prolonged or, worse, increased. That thought
bears repeating: Unhealthy dependent relationships are those
in which the person who leads behaves in ways that tend to
reinforce dependency, sometimes even making it permanent—
in effect, crippling the person who follows. For most of us, of
course, it's a matter of degree. We can't always be as nurturing as we'd like to be. No matter how exalted our intentions
are, we constantly run the risk of inadvertently injuring our
children, students, employees, anyone who needs us or relies
upon us. Life, as I said earlier, is a contact sport. Occasionally you'll step on the toes of others, just as they'll step on
yours. Usually the resulting damage is minor and reversible.
But because responsive parents, teachers, and managers possess more power, and thus greater ability to do harm, they
owe it to their children, students, and employees to be vigilant, paying very close attention to how they are actually af-
fecting others. Taking the lead requires that you be both lead

> *Dependent relationships become unhealthy when they needlessly prolong dependency.*

protector and lead problem-solver. Try to back up your words and actions with love—so that no matter what else is happening, you're always communicating concern and respect.

Also recognize when patience is needed. And never, never underestimate the practical effects of patience.

As the person who's leading, it's your job to provide the environment of encouragement that I outlined in Chapter 3, where I addressed the destructive influence of the inner critic. It's your job to create a playful, experimental atmosphere, in which stumbling isn't viewed as failure, in which those who follow are rewarded for trying, and trying again. Insisting that others be perfect is just as destructive as demanding it of yourself; and nurturing wholeness is just as constructive. When our children, students, and employees sense that their every move is being scrutinized, judged, held to an ideal standard, they feel suffocated. They become fearful and hesitant. They freeze up. The energy they need for the task at hand is diverted to worrying about possible missteps or regret for missteps that have already occurred but need to be forgotten.

In all that you do and say, project an attitude of acceptance, forgiveness, and empathy. Give those who depend upon you room to grow. Give them permission to be who they are right now while admitting to yourself that you don't know

> *Give those who depend upon you permission to be themselves.*

what they might be capable of by this time next year, or a month from now, or even within the hour. One of our most common mistakes is to underestimate others. If it becomes a habit, underestimating can turn into a self-fulfilling prophecy. Instead of empowering our children, students, and employees—making them feel *able* in our presence—we then *dis*able them. Let go of the little things. Don't nitpick. Make a habit of making other people feel worthy, capable, full of promise. You'll be surprised by the energy that's released when people are free to stumble, by the wonders that spring spontaneously from imperfection. In addition, try always to convey to others that their capabilities can only be discovered through action. For dependents to fulfill themselves in the dance of life, they must get out on the floor *and dance*. If they remain spectators they may avoid certain risks, but they'll also squander their birthright.

> *Make a habit of making others feel worthy, capable.*

While encouraging others to risk stumbling, it's easy to forget that *we* can also misstep. Leading is a skill like any other. It requires lifelong practice. Mistakes are inevitable—total mastery, impossible. And those who take the lead aren't immune from the inner critic. To maintain our own balance, especially when others are leaning on us for support, it's important to cultivate self-forgiveness, to resist succumbing to fear or doubt, to try and try again, just as if we were taking *our* first steps, even while showing and helping others take theirs. Perfection isn't the goal. Fulfillment is. If you've made a habit of criticizing

> *Leading is a skill like any other. Mistakes are inevitable— total mastery, impossible.*

your children, students, or employees, you've almost certainly fallen under the destructive influence of your own inner critic.

Even if you have subdued your inner critic, when you take the lead in a dependent relationship you always run the risk of projecting your picture of how things should be on the person who relies upon you for protection and guidance. The closer you are to that person, and the more you care about him or her, the greater the likelihood that this will happen. This is because of the tendency to identify with the fortunes of dependents, even, in extreme cases, to see his or her life as an extension of your own. But identifying with your dependent isn't always healthy or constructive. This may seem contradictory, after what I said above about the value of compassion. But I'm now referring to a special kind of identification, one that is less about empathy for someone else—who they are and what their circumstances may be—than it is about molding them into something other than who they are. Parents and teachers who identify in this way operate on the basis of *expectations* that are false, unrealistic, inappropriate, or otherwise out-of-sync. Instead of starting where their

> *Encourage your children to be what they want to be rather than impose your expectations, your pre-set ideas of what they should be.*

children and students are, then helping them to grow in their own way and at their own tempo, they try to get their dependents to conform to a pre-set plan. Rather than offer encouragement, they scold and disapprove, relying on words like *"shoulda," "woulda,"* and *"coulda:" You* shoulda *made a different choice. I* woulda *done it this way. You* coulda *been more like what I wanted you to be.*

A particularly unfortunate way that those in the lead impose their expectations on those who follow is by engaging in comparison. A teacher ridicules one student by praising the performance of another. A parent shames a younger sibling by comparing her behavior to that of an older one. This is always misguided. Why? The reasons are numerous but perhaps the easiest explanation stems from the distinction I made between perfection and wholeness. Recall that the pursuit of perfection cuts us off from parts of ourselves, as well as the world, because it doesn't allow for who we are at this moment and therefore doesn't make room for growth, learning, and practicing being human. The pursuit of wholeness, by contrast, assumes that every person is different, every person is *imperfect* in different ways. To become whole, to fill up your life space, is the same as becoming wholly who you are, in all your singularity. Carl Jung, the visionary psychologist who promoted the philosophy of wholeness, gave a name to this process: *individualization.* He considered it one of our highest callings. If you agree with Jung, as I do, then making

> *Every child's path to personal fulfillment, to becoming a whole individual, is unique.*

comparisons between people is absurd and, much worse, destructive, because it denies what's most valuable in each of us. Everyone's path to personal fulfillment, to become wholly individuated, is unique.

Maybe this goes without saying, but I'll say it anyway, to make sure the implications are clear: All of the foregoing applies as well to relationships between equals. To be sure, expectation is potentially more dangerous in parent-child and teacher-student relationships, on account of the heightened vulnerability of dependents, but it also can do a great deal of damage in marriages, friendships, work relationships, and so on. In a sense, Chapter 8, "Duets," is a primer on avoiding the pitfalls of expectation. But one aspect of the problem wasn't mentioned, and that's when our picture of how others should and could behave causes us to question their commitment to the relationship. Just as individual paths to wholeness differ greatly, so do the ways people show their love. Some are physically demonstrative. Others are verbal. Still others express themselves through what they do, make, or give. Recognizing and appreciating your partner's manner of expression, pertaining to love or any other emotion, is essential to the well-being and longevity of the partnership. The same is true of dependent relationships, in which the issue may not be the child's or student's commitment to the relationship per se but to the learning and development the relationship is supposed to cultivate. Never question someone's commitment merely

> *Never question a dependent's commitment to growth merely because his or her style of expression differs from yours.*

because their form of expression, including their style of behavior, differs from yours.

Besides valuing others for who they are and making room for them to develop in their own fashion, the best way to avoid the error of expectation is to remember the difference between taking responsibility for a relationship and taking responsibility for the other person's behavior. To be sure, in healthy dependent relationships, the person who leads carries more of the weight. This is especially true of the parent-child relationship, and most especially during the period from birth to adulthood. But since the overarching aim of the relationship is to foster increasing independence, over time the child should become increasingly responsible for his or her actions. That's one of the meanings of maturity, of course. More important, it's one of the meanings of freedom. People who can stand on their own two feet accept that they, not anyone else, are accountable for what they do. As parents, and as teachers, managers, and caregivers, we best serve the needs of those who depend on us by creating an environment that encourages them to take on ever more responsibility and—this is crucial—rewards them for doing so. We fulfill our roles by *holding them accountable*. This is how the person in the lead remains faithful to the relationship, to the long-term goal of fostering autonomy. Not by making excuses. Not by turning a blind eye to mistakes or bad behavior. And not by cleaning up

> *To foster independence in your children, you must hold them more and more accountable for their own behavior.*

the messes others make. The key to being an effective, constructive parent is knowing where to draw the line between your responsibility for the relationship and your child's accountability for his or her own behavior. As your son or daughter matures, the line will shift, which requires that you be both vigilant and flexible. It's certainly no easy task but one that must be taken very seriously.

Children mature mentally by mimicking and experimenting. They imitate over and over again—they *practice*—gradually getting closer to the desired behavior. Anyone who's witnessed a baby learn to talk can't help but be astounded by the process. In a remarkably short time, the child acquires an exceedingly sophisticated skill and, what's more, does so simply by repeating the sounds made by parents and others with whom they come into contact. (Note how most parents behave in this situation, never punishing missteps but always rewarding each and every step in the right direction, no matter how small.) The acquisition of language only appears to be simple, of course, and actually involves everything from genetic factors and neurological processes to cultural and other environmental influences. For our purposes, though, what deserves closer attention is the powerful role of imitation, not only in learning to talk but in all aspects of growth. The implications for those

> *The key to being an effective parent is knowing where to draw the line between your responsibility and your child's accountability.*

who take the lead in healthy dependent relationships are profound.

Remember that line of advice adults sometimes utter when their behavior doesn't measure up to the standard they're trying to set for their children: Do as I say, not as I do. Every time I hear it, I cringe. Once you appreciate the importance of mimicry in human development, you realize that this formula isn't likely to influence anyone's behavior. Truth be told, it's a pathetic distraction, designed to shift attention away from the adult. By contrast, effective parents, teachers, and managers always try to do the right thing because they know that children, students, and employees are much more likely *to do as they do*. That's how relationships work, and not just the dependent ones. Many experts in social psychology believe that what most inspires us to behave well are not general ethical prescriptions, such as, thou shalt not steal. To be sure, moral guidelines are necessary, but often more important in terms of actually influencing behavior is observing specific instances of other people behaving well. Cases range from the commonplace (a two-year-old boy sees his older brother helping his mother in the kitchen so he does the same) to the historically outstanding (an entire African American community mounts a city-wide boycott after hearing that one woman, civil rights pioneer Rosa Parks, refused to sit in the back of a segregated bus).

> *Always try to do the right thing because your children are much more likely to do as you do than do as you say.*

Teaching by example. Modeling. Walking the walk. No doubt you've heard at least one of these terms. Besides referring to the potential of particular acts to affect the behavior of others, they underscore something that's even more influential in ordinary day-to-day human affairs: *how* we go about meeting life's particular challenges. By that I mean our overall style of problem-solving, the *way* we handle difficulty and disappointment. If we don't always find the right solution, and none of us do or ever will, we can almost always *adopt the right approach* to finding the solution. And when we model the right approach, we enable those in our care to learn how to take care of themselves—to stand on their own. By right approach I mean the relationship principles I've already discussed, including those mentioned in this chapter, such as responsiveness, starting where your dependents are, giving them permission to be who they are, making room for them to make mistakes, making them feel worthy and capable, and so forth. Action that's consistent with these principles always speaks much louder—and is much more fruitful—than mere words.

> *The best way to nurture independence is to model the right approach to difficulty and disappointment.*

Putting imitation to good use also includes modeling behavior that counters the destructive modeling that may be taking place in other parts of your dependent's environment. Increasingly, children are exposed to influences outside the home. Indeed, after age six or so, many boys and girls spend more time at school, engaged in activities with friends, and preoccupied with television, the Internet, video games, and other high-tech devices than they do with their families. As every mother and father knows, electronic imagery is now so pervasive and so powerful that it sometimes seems like the media have taken over the role of parenting. This brave new world may seem to require brave new approaches but the same mentoring principles apply: *Encourage rather than disapprove. Allow children to be who they are, to make their own mistakes. Do as you want them to do, no matter how long it takes for them to appreciate it.* None of this is meant to suggest that you shouldn't express disagreement. But, even with young children, opposing points of view should be presented in respectful ways. Humiliating, haranguing, bullying—all of these are likely to yield the opposite of what's intended. You'll be more effective as a parent if you help your children to become independent, to forge their own identities and make their own choices, instead of obsessing over a particular behavior that you find disagreeable.

Focusing on modeling behavior will also help you walk the fine line between your responsibility and your dependent's accountability. Let's go back to the dance floor for an example. The most difficult tasks I've faced as an instructor don't involve dance per se. Basic dance skills are easy to teach, easy to learn. What makes instruction difficult is the psychological state of some students. One person might be agitated or angry while another is timid. Some people simply don't believe they can learn anything new; they feel neither capable nor worthy. Others are suspicious, finding it hard to trust or cooperate, or easily become

jealous when they see someone else succeed. Addressing these issues isn't the
first duty of a dance instructor, yet they
can't be ignored if dance instruction is to
be effective. Though I'm not responsible
for my students' behavior, I am responsible for *my relationships with my students*. I
take ownership of what we try to accomplish together but not for what they bring
to the dance floor as individuals. In practical terms this translates into modeling
constructive behavior—responsiveness,
patience, encouragement, and the like—while not making the
mistake of identifying with their destructive behavior. What I'm
then doing is demonstrating the proper problem-solving process
while addressing specific problems as they arise. It's up to each
student to pay attention to the process and adapt it to his or her
own life.

> *If you're leading in the dance of life, always model constructive behavior but never identify with the destructive behavior of those who are following.*

We should acknowledge that in the most extreme dependent relationships, those between parents and children, the
mother and/or father begin by assuming full responsibility for
their sons and daughters. An infant, after all, is helpless. But
gradually parental responsibility decreases. Children become
more independent and therefore more accountable for their
behavior. To varying degrees, the rhythm of responsibility and
accountability is a feature of every dependent relationship
in which independence is the long-term goal. And like the
rhythm of control and letting go, it also applies to equal relationships, in which both people are supposed to be able to

> ↶
> *Take responsibility for the relationship while holding your partner— and yourself— accountable for individual behavior.*

stand on their own feet from the start but, as everyone knows, often can't. The wisdom of combining relationship responsibility with individual accountability is its generosity. You essentially convey to your partner that you'll always encourage the best in him or her but never indulge their worst while remaining committed to the long-term well-being of the partnership.

Dependent relationships, however, differ in one fundamental way. If they follow their proper course, the dependency comes to an end. Children mature and leave home. Students outgrow their teachers. Employees become managers themselves, maybe moving to another company or starting one of their own. Patients get well; they go home. In all cases loss is inevitable, and the sense of loss is almost always more keenly felt by the parent, teacher, or caregiver. That's the hidden irony of leading. That's when you realize the extent to which you also had been dependent—on the relationship itself. Most of us need to take the lead in a dependent relationship to be able to be fulfilled as human beings. But with fulfillment comes heartache. Parents know this all too well—the pain of losing a relation-

> ↶
> *The final and most valuable gift you can give to your children is to no longer treat them as children.*

ship that has brought them great joy and satisfaction over many years. The final and most valuable gift you can give to your children is to no longer treat them as children—in other words, accept them and love them as independent people, free to move across the dance floor of life without you.

Letting go of those we love most and have cared for longest is one of life's most bittersweet moments.

ELEVEN

Dance of Departure

Movement never lies.

—MARTHA GRAHAM

ave you ever wondered why your heart swells up or tears suddenly pour forth when you say good-bye to a dear friend, family member, or loved one? Sure, you'll miss them, and anticipating the separation makes you sad. But what about those occasions when someone you care about is leaving only briefly, yet you still respond as if they'll be absent for a long time or are going far away? At one time or another, most of us have experienced this, being overcome with emotion for no apparent reason. And most of us have laughed it off. But I believe this seemingly trivial if inappropriate reaction is related to an aspect of the dance of life that all of

> *Every farewell is a reminder that nothing lasts forever.*

us fear. Every good-bye, no matter how routine, foreshadows the final good-bye. Every farewell is a reminder that nothing lasts forever, that every- thing we value most—a job; a special place, possession, or skill; our health; relationships with those we love—can end at any moment. *To every thing there is a season,* to borrow again the words of the biblical passage I cited earlier.

Whether or not you take the Bible as the revealed word of God, there's no question that it contains a great deal of wis- dom regarding the human condition—that sometimes life gives us blessings, other times it takes them away, and when it does so is determined mostly by forces larger than us. All of the world's major spiritual and philosophical traditions are in agreement on this point. Yet certain people would have us believe otherwise, promoting the view that we can acquire or achieve anything we wish merely by adopting the proper outlook or thinking about what we desire in the right way. As you'll recall, I certainly believe in cultivating a positive atti- tude, and I'm convinced that some thoughts are more ef- fective than others. But I hold these views for precisely the opposite reason: We can't always get what we want, which we need to acknowledge to be able to live as fully as possible. There's no magic formula for avoiding this hard truth. And if someone tells you differ- ently, keep an eye on your wallet, as well

> *Cultivate a positive attitude precisely because you can't always get what you want.*

as your common sense. The latest version of snake oil is about to be unveiled.

The success of thinking-makes-it-so hucksters depends entirely on your gullibility. In particular, it depends on your not being aware that the secret to getting what you want was revealed thousands of years ago, and it's not an easy pill to swallow. In the Buddhist tradition, its purest version, the secret goes like this: Desire itself is the source of all human suffering. The only way to avoid pain, frustration, and disappointment is to never want anything. It's as simple—and as harsh—as that. Give up your possessions; extinguish all ambitions and aspirations; detach yourself from everyone. After that, you'll be free of suffering because losing what isn't yours can't hurt you. Very few of us, of course, are suited for such a severe spiritual discipline. We're not going to withdraw from the world and lead a monkish existence of self-induced solitude and poverty. Given a choice between fulfilling some of our desires some of the time and not desiring anything at all, we'll gamble on the former. And deep

> *Desire always comes at a cost.*

down, we know that it is in fact a gamble, that every time we get attached to something or someone we risk experiencing pain. Desire always comes at a cost, though it's impossible to appreciate the true nature and full scope of the cost until the bill comes due.

When choreographer Martha Graham said that movement never lies she meant that it is what it is. A turn, jump, or other dance step doesn't pretend to be anything other than itself. Much the same is true of the basic moves in the life of a human

being, especially loss, and no loss speaks clearer than the death
of someone we love. Indeed, death, the final movement, is the
most brutally honest statement about existence you'll ever witness. What does it say? That one of the keys to human fulfillment, to filling our life space, is learning how to live with grace
and generosity *despite not always getting what we want.*

Here's another question: Have you ever noticed that we're
rarely puzzled when, out of the blue, *good* things happen? We
don't view lucky breaks as bizarre. When things go our way for
unknown reasons or due to no efforts of our own, we don't
worry that the natural order of things is
breaking down, that life is becoming unpredictable, chaotic. Yet this is exactly
how we tend to react to unexpected mis-
fortune: *I can't believe this is happening to
me. This can't be happening to me because
I'm a good and caring person. If this is
happening to me, then the world has gone
crazy.* This was more-or-less my outlook
when I was in my early thirties. Up until
that time, I'd been spared major disappointment. Nothing particularly grave had ever challenged my assumption that all
problems are fixable. There was no reason, I believed, why I
shouldn't be happy all the time. If I put my mind to it and gave
it my best effort, I could reach any goal I set for myself.

Then, as I like to say, life happened to me. My mother died.
She'd been in declining health for years, but no one in my family, least of all me, was prepared for the summer afternoon her
heart suddenly gave out and she collapsed to the kitchen floor

> *One key to
> fulfillment is
> living with grace
> and generosity
> despite not always
> getting what
> we want.*

of the home where I grew up. Back then, I was single, as well as single-minded, my work at the Fred Astaire studio not leaving much time for socializing. So it was Mom in whom I confided, to whom I turned for consolation and company, with whom I shared all my joys and triumphs. In short, she was my best friend as well as my mother.

Mom also was my biggest fan, taking great interest in everything I did as a dancer, dance instructor, and dance studio manager. From the start, she and Dad had been highly supportive. They bought me my first pair of dance shoes, putting the purchase on their credit card. They rooted for me when I competed. And they always made sure that I knew they were proud of me. But because of the special bond mothers and daughters sometimes form, and because Mom so thoroughly identified with any success I might experience in the dance world, my relationship with her was inseparable from my life as a dancer. She and Dad lacked the wherewithal to travel to my competitions. But whenever I performed, I imagined them in the audience, imagined their expressions as I turned across the dance floor. Among the most memorable occasions was the World Theatrical Dance Championships, held in 1984, at Madison Square Garden. The event was televised. I knew Mom was watching at home while my partner and I went on to place fifth in the Theater Arts Division, a more interpretive form of ballroom dancing, which includes many dramatic lifts. She was the first person I called afterward. That was one of the happiest days of my life, largely because I shared my achievement with her, and shared it while it actually happened. In a very real sense, it was *our* achievement. And at the time, it was unimaginable that a day would come when enjoying such moments together would no longer be possible.

When, twelve years later, that grim day did arrive, I was devastated, but I managed at first to maintain a certain level of composure. It helped greatly that I was immediately preoccupied with various obligations, from preparing for the funeral and burial to planning with my sisters and brothers how we'd make sure that Dad survived the ordeal and somehow began life anew. Being *actively* engaged in coping, and especially focusing on external problems, served as a refuge. And the same thing happened when I returned to the studio. It was a very demanding period. There were countless problems to be solved, tasks to be performed, events to be coordinated. So I plunged in, putting in as many hours as I possibly could. If you'd asked me at the time, I might've explained my obsession with work in terms of duty, responsibility. And that would've been true, but only partly. Something else was keeping me at the studio long after everyone else had left for the day: I dreaded going back to my house, dreaded being alone with nothing but my own thoughts and feelings. In my bones I knew that I hadn't yet faced the truth of *what had happened to me* as a result of what had happened to my mother.

The inevitable reckoning came one night while I was standing at the kitchen sink. Without warning, an immense wave of sorrow welled up inside me. My entire body was awash in pain. The next thing I knew, I was laying on the floor, sobbing uncontrollably. And there I stayed, stunned and helpless, for at least a half-hour. For the first time since Mom passed away, I let go of my roles as person-in-charge, person-who's-always-upbeat, person-who-never-gives-up. As a Fred Astaire studio manager and owner, I had created an identity based on analyzing and solving problems. I had no doubt that I could fix anything, large or small. But here was a problem for which no solution existed. At that moment, what I wanted most in the world was for my beloved mother to still be alive. I wanted to pick up the phone and call my sole confidant, the person I talked to every day since I had started dancing, the only person I ever needed to call. As a lifelong Catholic, I believe in an afterlife, and it's a great comfort to me. But even believers must come to terms with the *sense of finality* that accompanies the loss of a loved one. Emotionally speaking, no one is fully prepared for that. We may meet again in heaven, whatever that might actually mean. And life here on Earth may go on. But there's no denying that something of enormous value and significance has come to end and that *it will never be again.*

> *Everyone must come to terms with the sense of finality that accompanies the loss of a loved one.*

For me, laying on my kitchen floor, paralyzed with grief, the finality of my mother's departure took the form of a question that through the tears I asked myself repeatedly: Who can I now call? And again and again I heard the same answer: no one. Never have I felt more alone. And never has it been more painfully clear that solitude, dancing solo, may be the most difficult challenge we'll ever face.

It would be foolish to think that one loss, no matter how profound, provides a blueprint for all other losses we might

178

undergo. Every major loss is unique; every major loss forces us to dance solo to one degree or another. In other words, going it alone is an integral part of the experience. Each of us must find her own way to come to terms with what we've lost, which makes the idea of a how-to manual all the more absurd. But there are helpful principles to keep in mind. Taken together, these principles can serve as an overall framework for putting loss into perspective, giving you the means to orient yourself during times of great sorrow and uncertainty. Losing what we care about most *makes us feel lost*. It often threatens the foundations of our identity, especially how we picture ourselves and how we think life is supposed to work. It makes us feel estranged

> *Coming to terms with loss means learning how to feel at home in the world again.*

from the world, which in an instant becomes foreign and forbidding. To continue dancing wholeheartedly, which is the subject of the rest of this chapter and all of the next, we must somehow find our way back to life and the living so that we feel at home in the world again, so that our appetite for life is renewed.

One of the first principles in dealing with loss is that it's okay to leave the dance floor for a while. In fact, it's usually necessary. When you're severely hurt, you should take a break so that healing can occur. When the external world is spinning out of control, it's time to focus on the internal world, what's going on inside. Another principle that's helpful to remember early in the grieving process is that, despite what you may have read or what well-meaning people may tell you, the process doesn't unfold in

> -◁
> *After a major*
> *loss, it's okay to leave*
> *the dance floor*
> *for a while.*

an orderly, stepwise fashion. Grief, first and foremost, is chaotic. It's a condition marked by *disorder* and unpredictability. That's why it's important that we develop and maintain a framework for regaining our bearings.

Don't get me wrong. You'll almost certainly experience denial, anger, and the other so-called stages of grief. But don't count on them to adhere to any particular pattern. You may cycle through all of them several times a day. You may experience two of them at once, laughing and crying simultaneously. You may reach the acceptance stage one minute, then the next minute find yourself retreating into denial all over again. Being whipped back and forth emotionally, as if you were on a sadistic carnival ride, is what grief really feels like. But because it's so disorienting, so unlike ordinary

> -◁
> *Although grief*
> *makes you feel like*
> *you're dying, it*
> *won't kill you.*

day-to-day existence, it can seem unnatural, especially if you've never gone through it before. Worse still, it can seem as if you won't survive—that you'll either die or go insane. Again, this is natural. This is how grief works. Tell yourself that. Over and over. Add this to your list of mantras, as well: *Grief is awful, but it won't kill me.*

If you look very closely at the sensation of dying that accompanies grief, what you'll find is that any major loss is actually two losses: The death of a loved one, to use the most extreme example, and the death of the *relationship* with that loved one. And

> ~∅
>
> *When we lose someone we love, we also lose the relationship we enjoyed with that person.*

where is that relationship located? To a great extent, it's inside you. It's part of the fabric of your being. It's who you are. Remember, as social animals, we are defined to a large degree by our relationships. We shouldn't be surprised, then, that we feel as if we're dying when those we love are taken from us.

Truth be told, something *is* dying, something deep within, something of immense significance. Recognizing that, learning to accept it, is as important to the grieving process as recognizing and accepting that a particular parent, spouse, child, relative, or friend is gone and will never return.

Those of us who enjoy relatively stable, comfortable lives in the United States can count ourselves lucky that we experience loss as little as we do. Most people in the world don't have the luxury of reading a book like this because they have all they can do to survive from one day to the next. But we pay a price for our privileges in that we are poorly prepared for the dark side of life. One of our most naive notions is that bad things aren't supposed to happen to good people. Another is that we're entitled to be happy, that happiness is under our control. You may have noticed that until now I haven't said anything about happiness per se. That was deliberate. Making happiness a long-term goal is very much like making perfection a long-term goal. In my experience, happiness arrives as a byproduct, or extra benefit, of other pursuits—primarily, the pursuit of wholeness and fulfillment. It's no accident that the happiest people in the world are those who don't think about their own happiness at all but instead tend to the needs of others. Give up the vain pursuit of happiness so that you may give yourself to your family, a worthy occupation, the betterment of some portion of the world. That's when, wonder of wonders, happiness is most likely to grace your life.

> *Happiness comes as an extra benefit of pursuing wholeness and fulfillment.*

Losing what we care about most isn't easy for anyone, but the best prepared are those who appreciate the ebb and flow of existence. The dance of life is a dance of give and take. If you don't know that, if you don't accept it, the pain you experience will be compounded. This is what I meant earlier about losses threatening the very foundation of identity. If your sense of self and how

> *If you understand and respect the give-and-take of life, losing what you love won't knock you off-balance.*

the world works is based on faulty ideas—and nothing could be faultier than the belief that you can force the world to do your bidding—then the death of a loved one may make you feel like you're losing your mind. The world will seem all the stranger and more chaotic. If, on the other hand, you truly understand and respect life's give-and-take rhythm, you will still suffer but the suffering won't knock you off-balance. It won't imperil your ability to stand on your own two feet and continue dancing. You'll be more graceful, more generous. You'll possess the strength and wisdom *to stop clinging to things that are gone.*

I say this as someone who wasn't well-prepared for the first big loss of her life. Up until my mother's death, I looked at everything through rose-colored glasses. When I lost her, the glasses came off. For the first time, I was forced to view life as it is, rather than what I imagined it to be or believed it was sup-posed to be. When I say *life as it is* I'm not suggesting that we adopt an atti-tude of fatalism or defeat. Not in the least. All along, I've stressed the im-portance of action, taking steps, dis-covering the limits to your life space through experimentation and prac-tice. But I am saying that you stand a much better chance of *creating* a life that's fruitful and fulfill-ing if you start by respecting life as it is, which in this case means the give-and-take that is the pulse of existence. Remem-ber the sailboat metaphor? What I'm calling give-and-take is the equivalent of wind and water currents. If the pilot fails to read those currents correctly, the boat won't get anywhere. It's the same in life. Learn to read the currents. Then learn to make those currents work for you.

> *Learn to read the currents of life, then learn to make the currents of life work for you.*

One of the lessons I learned about the give-and-take of life following my mother's death is that I wouldn't have been so eas-ily knocked off-balance had I developed a wide range of nurtur-ing, constructive relationships. As I've said, every major loss throws us back on our own resources, challenges who we are, forces us to come to terms with harsh realities *alone*. But my dancing solo needn't have been as extreme and unrelieved as it was. Losing Mom was a paralyzing loss because I relied almost exclusively upon my relationship with her to satisfy all of my basic relationship needs. Loving her as much I did wasn't a mistake, but expecting so much of our relationship certainly was. That's why I couldn't stand on my own, why I literally lost my footing and fell to the floor.

At the time I didn't understand what was happening, of course. It took all of my strength to keep from crawling into bed and staying there. But eventually what dawned on me are the central themes of this book—that we are our relationships and because of that we need many different kinds of relationships to become fully realized human beings. A practical advantage of this approach is that the more fully realized you are, the better prepared you'll be for loss of any kind, including the death of loved ones. Sometimes your primary partner isn't going to be there to catch you. When that happens, it'll be much easier for you to continue dancing, to avoid paralysis, if you have a balanced life, rich with gratifying activities and nurturing relationships.

> *We need many different kinds of relationships to become fully realized human beings.*

Another reason why my mother's passing shook the foundations of my existence is that I believed it happened much too soon, before we had a chance to enjoy together some of life's outstanding moments. Besides grieving for her and for our relationship, I grieved for what *might have been.* I now realized that, among other disappointments, she wouldn't see me get married, have children, or advance any further in the dance business. Anyone who's experienced the death of a loved one, the destruction of some beloved place or possession, or the premature end to a labor of love knows that the loss of what-might-have-been inflicts an especially cruel kind of pain. You feel betrayed by life. You feel that whatever meaning life once held has been stolen from you. The loss seems so overwhelmingly unfair that you risk being consumed by anger or despair. This sorrowful state has an illuminating parallel in the world of competitive dance—when a couple isn't called back for the next round. Everyone works extremely hard to reach the competitive level. Everyone sacrifices, endures much pain, puts the same effort into practice and preparation. Yet some don't receive a call back. I've seen young couples quit dancing after missing only one or two callbacks. I've also seen couples continue dancing for years despite never getting called back after the first round.

Why do some persist, and others not? I can't speak for everyone, of course. But the couples I know who aren't deterred by rejection have one crucial characteristic in common: They enjoy the process as much or more than the potential outcome. In other words, they dance to be dancing instead of to be winning. They fulfill themselves as dancers every actual moment they're dancing, not by reaching an imaginary moment in the future. They're fully present and wholly engaged in the here-and-now. How these couples handle not receiving callbacks has much to teach us about dancing through life, in particular, how to continue dancing after losing what-might-have-been. If in

> *Bringing each moment to fulfillment is what matters most.*

your relationships—indeed, in all that you do—you seek wholeness rather than perfection, you'll be better equipped to appreciate that all losses come too soon, because life itself is incomplete and unfinished. Life, like love and being human and everything else in the universe, is a work in progress. Or, to put it in more personal terms, if you're giving yourself wholly to your relationships, bringing each moment to fulfillment is what matters most. Adopting this approach won't free you entirely from being haunted by what-might-have-been. But it'll help you maintain your balance during the onslaught.

Fortunately, when I came home after Mom died I had a business to run. Staying in bed wasn't an option. Withdrawing from the world to dwell on what-might-have-been was out of the question. I had to pull myself up off the floor and go to work. That led to the new management philosophy that I've already described. It also led to a reassessment of my resources, both internal and external. Before losing my mother, I had thought that my most valuable internal resource was energy and that my most valuable external resource was love (in my personal life) or money (in my professional life). But I was wrong about the latter. My most valuable external resource is time. *Your* most valuable external resource is time. And once you grasp that, you also grasp that nothing is more important than how you use your energies in the time you're allowed, including the time that follows the departure of a loved one. The dance of life will continue. No matter how weak, even disabled, you may feel at first, it's always within your power to join in again.

> *Nothing is more important than how you use your energies in the time you're allowed on the dance floor of life.*

TWELVE

Back on the Dance Floor

I have discovered the dance.
—ISADORA DUNCAN

What I said about happiness toward the end of the last chapter may have struck you as odd and maybe a little frustrating. Not only is the pursuit of happiness the bread and butter of most self-help books, it's one of the "unalienable rights," along with life and liberty, that our forefathers enshrined in the Declaration of Independence. What loyal, level-headed American would oppose that?

Let me be absolutely clear: I don't oppose the pursuit of happiness. I desire happiness just as much as anyone else. And I want others to be happy, especially those I love and care about most. What I oppose are ideas about the pursuit of happiness that are more comforting than useful. I could do what some do, tell you a pretty fairytale that lulls you into believing that life is a breeze. I could claim that I've discovered a secret formula for curing all your ills, satisfying all your needs. But that would be a waste of my time, and time, as I hope I've made clear, is my most precious resource. What's more, passing off fairytales and magic formulas as helpful advice would be a terrible disservice to you. I try instead to adopt a pragmatic approach, which, as you'll recall, measures all ideas by their effectiveness, by how fruitful there are. And the notion that you can will yourself to happiness just doesn't work. It's the wrong tool for the job.

One of the more obvious reasons it doesn't work is that it's usually based on the assumption that pain is unnecessary, avoidable, even that it can be eliminated altogether. Shortly before my father died—a loss I was better prepared for—he made a comment that I'll never forget: *"Everyone lives in pain."* Dad said it matter-of-factly. And that was the point. Pain is a fact of life. No big deal. Pretending that you can move across the dance floor of life without experiencing pain may ease your mind temporarily, but it won't reduce the pain that's sure to come. Most regrettably, it'll actually render you less capable of withstanding pain, of dancing through and be-yond pain. If you're going to live, you're going to get bumped and bruised. Short of being shot full of narcotics, the only pain-less state is the one that's available at the cemetery. And we'll all arrive there soon enough. I can't imagine anything worthwhile

> *Everything worthwhile in life requires sacrifice, and sacrifice is painful.*

that can be achieved without some measure of sacrifice, and sacrifice is painful. That's the definition of sacrifice: You give up something you want for something that you want more or that means more to you. Yes, happiness may come to those who persist, those who remain committed to a marriage, an occupation, or a long-term project of one sort or another, but only because of a process that itself isn't always or mostly pleasurable.

Unworkable prescriptions for achieving happiness often depend on another belief that doesn't square with experience—that disappointment, thwarted desire, loss, and the like are "problems" to be solved rather than inescapable aspects of human existence. Take the most extreme instance of loss—death. What might a solution to death look like? Even saying it that way sounds silly, doesn't it? Yet sometimes we behave as if we could "solve" death. The first rule of effective problem-solving is to describe the problem accurately. And in the case of death and other major losses, the problem isn't loss as such. The problem is *how we deal with loss*. Those who accept that the dance of desire and the dance of departure are actually two stages of the same dance are better equipped to undergo loss with grace and generosity. Desire is what propels us forward, outward. It connects us to the things of the world. It energizes us, carries us into the flow of life. But the things of the world, the things we get attached to, come and go. That's the rhythm of life. Major losses, and most especially the loss of a loved one, remind us that we

> *The dance of desire and the dance of departure are two stages of the same dance. You can't have one without the other.*

can't have one part of that rhythm without the other. We can't enjoy the dance of desire without also experiencing the dance of departure.

*A*fter you've recovered sufficiently from the initial shock of a major loss, getting back on the dance floor of life may require a burst of energy that you don't seem to possess. Taking the first small step down the line of dance may look to you like leaping over a broad, bottomless canyon. As with grief itself, it helps to have a way to put this situation into proper perspective. And it's at precisely this point that you'll need to draw on the power of positive thinking. When I say positive thinking, I don't mean thinking that, abracadabra, yields specific end results. I mean thinking that gets you moving again. It might help to picture it this way: The process is the result, just like the process of trying and trying again is the whole point of learning to walk. You don't learn how to walk by willing yourself to walk. You learn how to walk by taking the first step, stumbling, then, despite your awkwardness and incompetence, taking another step. By testing the limits of the possible through doing. By seeking fulfillment, or filling your life space, rather than chasing the mirage called perfection.

Positive thinking is thinking that leads to action, that gets you moving again.

One of most disabling sensations you'll experience in the wake of a major loss is that *life is happening to you*. The experience is stunning. It immobilizes you, mentally and physically. No longer do you feel like an active agent in the world, someone who takes a stand, who leads with one foot, who dances with conviction. You're now a passive victim. At least that's how it feels, a feeling that can be quite convincing, even if it's not true. And, believe me, it's not true. So the problem of how to deal with loss is in large part the problem of becoming an active agent again—of mustering up the courage and imagination to take that first step toward rediscovering the dance of life.

Fortunately, the dynamic that brought you to grief—the rhythm of desire and departure—is your best guide back to the dance floor. Just as desire leads to departure, so can departure lead to desire again if, that is, you permit yourself to make mistakes, ignore the inner critic, develop your own cheering section, seek situations in which experimentation is supported, and so on. In other words, getting back on your feet following an immobilizing loss or disappointment is very much like learning to walk all over again. It requires practice and persistence. Missteps are not only inevitable, they should be seen as successes. Always.

> *Just as desire leads to departure, so does departure lead back to desire.*

Remember that life, like dance, is movement, relationship in movement. *Relationship* and *movement*. Although how we go about relating and moving again can assume countless forms, it always entails energy flowing forward. That's your lifeline, your line of dance. *Life never flows backward.* But because, as human beings, we are blessed with a highly developed memory, we also have the ability to resist the flow of life by *looking backward,* focusing on the past, sometimes to the extent that we become blind to or estranged from the present. This suggests another way to think about dealing with loss: It's also a problem of attention, more precisely, of shifting attention away from the past, back to what's immediately in front of us. I'm not sug-

> *Shifting attention from the past to what's in front of you is necessary to getting back on the dance floor.*

gesting that this happens easily, or quickly, or that when it does happen, it happens permanently. But turning around and looking forward is necessary to getting back on the dance floor and once again following our line of dance.

Toward the end of the last chapter, I mentioned ways to become better prepared for loss and disappointment, in particular by recognizing and learning how to read the rhythmic give-and-take of existence as well as by cultivating a wide array of constructive relationships and making each and every moment count, all of which are necessary to fulfillment anyway. Another way to maintain balance during times of trouble is to have already developed the habit of beginning again. If you've made a lifelong practice—there's that word again—of renewing yourself through learning new skills, meeting and befriending new people, trying new experiences, and investigating new places, you'll have all the more reason to believe

> *Make a habit of starting over, of learning and doing new things. This will make it easier for you to keep your balance during times of trouble.*

that you're capable of starting over. You'll know what it *feels like* to start over.

In dance we call this muscle memory. Movements that have been well-practiced are actually recorded in the muscles. So even if you haven't danced in a long time, the movements soon come back and without your needing to think about it. Your body does the remembering. Similarly, if you've made a habit of sampling all that life has to offer, you'll instinctively look for and take advantage of opportunities to return to the dance floor. Or, to use a different metaphor, you'll be more likely to respond swiftly and confidently when the wind suddenly shifts, threatening to overturn your sail-boat. Let's stay with that second meta-phor a little longer because it points to something else that comes with making a habit of starting over. Note that the boat won't move without wind and water cur-rents, a condition at sea known as the doldrums. Sailing the boat depends on

> ‑◌
> *When you've been immobilized by loss, try to connect to something larger than yourself, something that will pull you back into the flow of life.*

external forces as much as it does on the efforts of the pilot. Here's the parallel: Starting over, especially starting over after losing a loved one, is often very difficult, if not impossible without additional energy from the outside. To overcome the doldrums that set in after we've been immobilized, we need to connect to something larger than ourselves, something that will *pull us back into the flow of life.*

That larger something varies from one person to the next and depends on circumstance. But as social creatures, we flow easiest by flowing with others. So the network of relationships that I mentioned earlier certainly qualifies. If you play multiple roles, and each role is fulfilling in its own way, you'll be in a better position to recover from the loss of any one particular role. Had I been married and with a family, as I am now, my mother's death probably wouldn't have knocked me off my feet. I might not have made the mistake of confusing my will to live with the will to live with Mom always by my side. That relationship, as important as it was, could have been part of a bigger, more complete, more balanced picture. Indeed, *I* could have been bigger, in the best sense of the word—largeness of spirit, or magnanimity, which is what enables us to be graceful and generous in the face of all manner of change, both positive as well as negative. When you have a family, of course, you're responsible for those who depend upon you. You have to be *responsive* to them, which in turn enlivens you, makes you more alive to the world. Sometimes nothing so readily heals a broken heart than caring for others.

> *If you play multiple roles, and the roles are fulfilling, you'll be better prepared for the loss of any one particular role.*

> *Sometimes the best cure for a broken heart is caring for others.*

The larger something that draws us back onto the dance floor could also be a community of like-minded friends, lifelong calling, constructive enterprise that you share with others over a long period of time, the wonder and solace of the natural world, or, of course, a higher spiritual power. In addition to providing the extra energy that's needed to overcome immobilization, surrendering to one of these larger somethings tends to induce a sense of gratitude. That's because your focus has shifted from what has departed to what still exists, what is *still desirable*. It's also because any loss makes you keenly aware of your own mortality. Life itself seems more vivid and therefore more precious. And as a consequence, *you* feel more vivid, *your* life more precious. It is as if you were being reborn, reawakening to the world. In the course of rediscovering the dance of life, you also renew yourself. This feeling might be fleeting. But it's a sure sign that you're ready to begin again, that you already have begun again.

Rediscovering the dance of life brings about self-renewal.

I don't want to overstate the notion of being reborn. By the time we reach adulthood, habits good and bad are well-established. Certain features of our character are all but permanently cast. Radical shifts in direction require radical shifts in perspective. That said, however, losing something or someone we care deeply about does in fact create conditions that favor a certain amount of change. For a short period, while you're taking your first steps after getting back on the dance floor, small opportunities open up, opportunities to alter the way you dance through life.

One of the things I discovered, and it's connected to my comments about time being my most valuable resource, is that by the time I reached my thirties my life had gotten filled with superficialities. I was distracted by numerous pointless activities. Although it may sound cruel to say this, I also suddenly realized I was in nonnurturing relationships with people I didn't really like or want to be around. And it became clear that I was devoting too much energy to little things and too little to big ones. Though I took pride in my ability to solve problems, and I excelled at it, I hadn't developed the ability to judge which problems most deserved my attention. So, after I got back on my feet, I started sorting through and disposing of the clutter. One of the principles that came out of this much-needed housecleaning phase is this: Just because you can, doesn't mean you should. Dancing through life is a series of small steps—a series of choices about where and how to move. Every moment is an opportunity. And every moment is a trade-off: You decide to do this activity rather than that one. You choose to be with one person instead of another. You try to focus your attention on what matters most at any particular time, not allowing yourself to be sidetracked or drained by the endless array of other things competing for your interest.

> *Just because you can, doesn't mean you should.*

What matters most is, of course, dictated by your long-range goals. That's another matter that arose after my mother died. Being reminded in such a dramatic way of the impermanence of life, including my own impermanence, forced me to reexamine the overarching goals that were supposed to be guiding my day-to-day goals. That's when I realized that I hadn't taken my own health seriously enough. Even after I retired from competition, I continued to dance, especially in Fred Astaire–related exhibitions. And I jogged and in-line skated

> *Everything you want to do will depend on maintaining a high level of energy.*

regularly. Consequently, I was in better-than-average shape. But there was so much more I could have done to improve my health. And now I was highly motivated. Sure, vanity played a part. I wanted to look good. But vitality was much more important. And the key to vitality is the concept I introduced back in Chapter 6: Energy is the essence of life. Everything I wanted to do from that moment forward would depend on my being able to maintain a high level of energy.

Remember what I said about muscle memory? Normally we think of memory as residing in the brain. And it surely does. But it also resides in the body, though only after a great deal of repetition, performing the same movements over and over again. To dancers this comes naturally. It's an occupation. More than that, it's a way of life. Even the most skilled, accomplished dancers in the world continue to *practice*, sometimes on a daily basis. For hours and hours, they repeat the same routines. This is how they stay fit, limber, strong. But it's also how they *absorb* those routines. When a dance is completely absorbed by the muscles and joints and other parts of the body, when it becomes who dancers are as physical beings, they no longer have to think about what they're doing. They are then free to give themselves completely to the rhythms and movements of the dance. All of their energy is

> *Focus on vitality instead of vanity.*

concentrated on the present, on each moment as it flows into the next.

The lesson in this for nondancers concerns the power of habitual behavior. Developing habits usually is an unconscious process. We acquire them without being aware of the fact. This is unfortunate in the case of bad habits because it means that by the time we do become conscious of the habits, they're deeply ingrained. We've "memorized" them so thoroughly that they're automatic. They have a life of their own. And when the most destructive habits—fear, doubt, anger, greed, lust for power—take on lives of their own, they cause all kinds of havoc. They destroy balance. They throw us out of sync with the dance of life. Our reactions to what happens around us are inappropriate or disproportionate. We can't read, still less adjust to the give-and-take of existence. Nor can we be responsive to others, and thereby responsible for our relationships, because instead of paying attention to our spouse, child, friend, or coworker, paying attention to *where they are at the time*, we're under the spell of negative emotions. Our energy is misdirected, dissipated.

Fortunately, the process by which habits are acquired can be used to our advantage. I've already discussed how to remedy destructive habitual behavior. What I want to examine here is the unique situation you'll find yourself in after undergoing profound loss, when you're given a chance to develop new habits, habits that could be more constructive than some of your old habits. You're about to take your first new step on the dance floor. Is there anything you'd like to do differently this time around? You had been convinced by your anguish that you would die or go crazy. But you did neither. You survived some-

> *After surviving a major loss, you have an opportunity to develop new, more constructive habits.*

thing you didn't believe was survivable. Now you're starting over. So pause for a moment, take a deep breath, and consider the big picture. Think of long-range character goals. What kind of person do you want to be? More caring? More forgiving? More tolerant? More flexible? Which day-to-day behaviors—behaviors that are doable for you—would be consistent with your revised picture of yourself?

I realize that I'm making this sound much easier—and more predictable—than it actually is. But if you start small, very small, then build slowly and consistently, it's possible to master new moves in the dance of life. Adopt a pragmatic attitude. View your attempt to develop different behaviors as an *experiment,* not a revolutionary change but merely a modest exercise that you'll continue until it yields whatever results it may yield. Learning a new move in life is very much like learning to walk. Be persistent. Accept stumbling as a necessary part of the process. Use all the techniques I've described for reducing the influence of the inner critic. Be sure to seek and create social circumstances in which your efforts will be encouraged and rewarded. And in keeping with that, don't be bashful about telling others how you wish to be treated. That's another lesson I took away from the experience of profound loss: My chances of getting what I desire increase significantly if I tell the world what I desire. This straightforward approach also has the advantage of saving time. You discover quickly whether you're in the right relationship, whether you should look for a different job, whether your neighborhood really matches your social, cultural, or recreational interests.

Lastly, model your experiment in new behavior after those virtuoso dancers who never cease practicing. Anything repeated often enough and consistently enough will become habitual. And sometimes a single small step in the right direction is all that's needed to create enough momentum to continue taking steps. One of the reasons ballroom dancing is so popular is that the immediate pleasure it provides is self-reinforcing. In other words, *the more you dance, the more you want to dance.* The same thing can happen in the dance of life, especially after you've suffered a great loss or disappointment, when your hunger for life is diminished, if not extinguished altogether. One little taste can rekindle your interest, making you want another taste, and still another, until your full hunger returns. Appetite, as the French say, grows by eating. That's the moment when you move from the dance of departure back to the dance of desire.

> *If you start small, adopt an experimental attitude, and persist, you can develop new habits.*

> *Sometimes one small step in the right direction is all that's needed to develop a new habit.*

$\int$ *nergy is the essence of life.* I can't stress that enough. Everything we do involves the creation, movement, conversion, or

> *The more you dance through life, the more you want to dance through life.*

exchange of energy, whether we're dancing solo, as a duet, or in concert with many others. And so it is with individual attempts to engage in more constructive behavior. Energy that's needed to develop a new habit has to come from somewhere, and often it's diverted from a bad habit, which weakens that habit's hold on you. The more you dance in a new way, the more you want to continue dancing that way, gradually reducing the energy and time available for dancing the old way.

Another aspect of human energy dynamics during times of trouble is the phenomenon of release. My mother was of Irish ancestry on both sides. So it seemed entirely fitting and deeply respectful of her spirit to say farewell in the customary manner, which, as you may know, calls for as much laughter as weeping. A proper Irish wake blends celebration with

> *There is life after death— your life.*

mourning. And the combination can be surprisingly liberating. Black humor, delivered with love and mischievous wit, lifts the weight of grief. It lightens the heart. It creates a surge of energy, releasing you from your pain. The sensation lasts only a moment, but that's long enough, if you're paying attention, to catch a glimpse of what awaits you after the anguish comes to an end, long enough to realize that there *is* indeed life after death— *your life.*

THIRTEEN

The Dance of Your Life

The dance is my being here in this space,
totally, and preparation for this performance is
my entire life and nothing more or less.

—DEBORAH HAY

Those of us who routinely buy and read self-help books, and I'm one of them, have one weakness in common: We keep searching for easy answers. But we really know better, don't we? There are no fail-safe formulas, no quick fixes. Just as a person cannot be all things to all people, or even to one person, neither can a book.

What I've described represents a certain point of view that's based on a certain set of experiences, in particular, my experiences in the world of dance. Some parts may be more useful to you than others. Your background, your experience, and your current position in life will dictate what's relevant and

> *Make a habit of listing your blessings and saying a prayer of thanks every day.*

what's not. And as noted earlier, the book as a whole doesn't offer much to those who endure extreme, prolonged forms of suffering, such as crushing poverty, domestic violence, political oppression, war, and so forth. It's crucial that we always keep in mind our less fortunate neighbors on the planet. Being fully alive and responsive means recognizing the pain of others, also that our pain is probably modest by comparison. In short, we're lucky. Very lucky.

The chief implication of such responsiveness is that the proper approach to life as a whole is a combination of gratitude and humility. Existence owes you nothing. But you owe it everything—you owe it your life, you owe it all the privileges you enjoy, including the privilege of being able to sit in peace and comfort, reading a book about personal development. Make a habit of listing your blessings and saying a prayer

> *Give yourself wholeheartedly to the dance of life.*

of thanks every day. That's your birthright. A wondrous thing. But it won't last. What are you going to make of it in the time that you're given, which isn't much time at all? Will you sit on the sidelines complaining, accusing, fearful or doubtful, nursing injuries or grievances, or will you get out on the dance floor? Will you hesitate, withhold yourself, squander your birthright, or will you give yourself wholeheartedly to the dance of life?

I've made many suggestions regarding how to take the first

steps and how to go about moving across the dance floor—how to dance through life with grace and generosity. If you're a student of self-help books, some of these principles surely sound familiar, even though they may be cast in somewhat unfamiliar terms. Others

> *Always picture yourself as an active, creative agent in the world.*

probably don't. Perhaps the principles that you find strangest are that *ideas should be treated as tools* instead of rock-solid truths, and that *being human is something you practice*, rather than something fixed and well-defined beforehand, something that you are, simply by virtue of being alive. My aim in promoting these principles is to stress *action* (we are active agents in the world) and *creativity* (we fulfill our potential primarily through taking action).

I do this not because I believe anything and everything is possible. That's a cruel hoax perpetrated by people who either aren't paying attention to how the world actually works or are pandering to the fears and doubts that plague all of us. By contrast, I stress an active, creative way of being because I believe that what's possible can't be known ahead of time, that the limits to our potential are to be determined through experimentation—in other words, through *practice*. Humanity is a work in progress. Life itself is a work in progress. I've found that this point of view is greatly empowering. It energizes me. It thrusts me into the stream of life—down what I call my line of dance. But it does so without making me Pollyannaish

> *Humanity is a work in progress. You are a work in progress.*

about the cruelties and disappointments of existence, and thus susceptible to being knocked off my feet when things don't go the way I want them to.

In my experience both on and off the dance floor, I've also found that taking action eventually shapes character. What we do, the gradual accumulation of countless tiny acts, determines to a great degree who we are. That's why I emphasize behavior—bringing it to light, reforming it if need be, as well as developing new behaviors, new ways of doing things. And in doing so, keep in mind, always occurs within the context of relationships. Essentially, this is an *ecological* way of looking at the human condition. Each of us is but one small part of a vast, exceedingly complex web of interdependent relationships. What's more, the web is constantly

> *Action shapes character.*

changing, evolving, each of its myriad parts modifying all the others to one degree or another.

If you respect both the fundamental reality of relationships and that relationships are always in motion, you'll be better equipped to read the give-and-take of existence, as well as to make the give-and-take work for you—to flow with the Flow, including during times of great disappointment or profound loss. From an ecological perspective, it also becomes clear why there are limits to the self-help model of human change. Some problems—poverty, oppression, and the like—can't be addressed effectively by individuals or pairs of individuals acting in isolation.

A brief list of informative books that explore ways to address collective problems can be found in the Appendix. The books include dozens upon dozens of inspirational stories about ordinary people making a difference in their communities. I recommend that you check out at least one of them, or one like them, if for no other reason than to see that there are other ways of thinking about the world we live in and the challenges it poses. Although the problems the books address are beyond the reach of *Dancing Through Life,* the overall approach they prescribe is consistent with the ideas at the core of my training philosophy: *Persistence is beauty. We're in this together. Goals provide direction. Respect is wisdom in action. Generosity is gratitude in action. Responsiveness is the soul of responsibility. Make a habit of starting over. Always picture yourself as an active, creative agent in the world. Humanity is a work in progress.* All of these principles apply as well to collective attempts to solve social and political ills.

One of this book's principles is especially relevant: *Take a stand.* As I pointed out in Chapter 4, "Dance of Desire," living with conviction creates energy. It causes movement, thrusting us onto the dance floor of life. And movement—taking action— is what brings about behavioral change. Conviction, in other words, is necessary for personal growth and fulfillment. But it's also essential to the well-being of neighborhoods, communities, and societies—if, that is, you believe that a robust, self-correcting democracy is the best of all possible political systems. Much of what's wrong with our country, as well as others, be they democratic or not, comes about and persists only because it's tolerated. There's a maxim that's often cited in this regard. To parapharse Edmund Burke: All it takes for evil to triumph is for good men to do nothing. By not taking a

> *Taking a stand also means standing up for what's right—freedom and justice.*

stand, we risk losing what we value most about America. Think of it this way: Just as individuals must adjust their short-term goals to keep their day-to-day lives aligned with their long-term goals, so too does a society need to make small course corrections so that it's always heading toward its destination, which in the United States is embodied in the words *freedom* and *justice*. The needed course corrections will take place only if individual citizens take a stand—if they stand up for what's right when what's right is imperiled.

The stories of social activists fighting for freedom and justice call attention to two other ideas that I believe everyone should keep in mind, no matter where they choose to direct their energy. The first is that many people discover they can't fully realize their potential as individuals until they devote themselves to a larger cause. Personal fulfillment comes through public service. Such service can assume a range of forms: participation as an individual citizen, involvement in local charitable functions, government service, or social activism. If you've taken to heart what I said about recovering

> *For some people, personal fulfillment comes through public service.*

from loss and bringing your personal dance into sync with the overall dance of life, this shouldn't seem paradoxical. Indeed, in its broadest form, the principle that we are our relationships implies the same thing: From the development of identity to personal destiny, everything about us is determined largely within a social context. So it stands to reason that the most inclusive social contexts—society as a whole, the world community, and humanity—play an important part in shaping all of our lives. The only questions are whether as individuals we're paying attention to the effects of those contexts and whether we wish to engage them in a conscious, creative way.

The second universal idea that arises from the experience of social activism is that the process must be as fulfilling as reaching the desired outcome. If you adopt a long view of the human experiment, taking into account all of recorded history, you realize that significant change is slow. Sometimes it's so slow that, from the standpoint of an individual life, it may seem impossible. How, then, can we set our sights on such lofty long-term goals as expanding the circle of freedom and creating a more just world? Aren't we condemning ourselves to failure, disappointment, and bitterness? If we're living only for the results, that imaginary moment in the future when all is achieved, then the answer is yes, decidedly yes. If, however, we're fully present and wholly engaged in *this* moment and in *this* place, the answer is no, of course not. And wholly engaged means being wholly engaged with other people. Again, instead of striving for perfection—which, in this case, is the day when freedom and justice reign supreme everywhere and for all time—we would do better to strive for wholeness. And that will come through our relationships with others who share our convictions, who stand with us when we take a stand, with whom we can share the satisfaction of incremental change. Solidarity, in short, makes the effort

THE DANCE OF YOUR LIFE

> *In efforts to bring about social change, as in personal growth, the process should be as fulfilling as reaching the desired outcome.*

worthwhile, makes the process fulfilling.

I'm aware that, by introducing such heavy subjects as freedom and justice, I've led you through a dance you probably didn't anticipate, and may have declined had you seen it coming. I appreciate your patience. As I've already stated, I believe that we're more likely to realize our potential as individuals if we're honest about the way the world actually works, then take action to make it work for us. Only those who indulge in illusion can experience disillusionment. Equally important, I believe that the more acquainted we become with the overall human condition—the story of humankind's struggle to make a better life on Earth—the more humble and forgiving we'll become. All human beings are in the same boat. All want safety and physical comfort, love, meaning, the satisfaction of being useful to others, and so on. Not all get what they want. And everyone, to quote my father again, lives in pain, some more so than others. Looking across the dance floor of life, I'm sometimes overwhelmed with feelings of tenderness and sympathy for my fellow dancers.

Looking across the dance floor, I'm also all the more appreciative of dance per se. And now I'm speaking literally, not metaphorically. I'm referring to the waltz, swing, or tango. Admittedly, dancing is a modest activity, one that for most people will never become more than a parttime recreational pursuit.

But I know of no other recreational activity that offers so many benefits to such a wide array of people.

Let's return to the basic physical and mental benefits, some of which I described back in Chapter 6. What I didn't mention is that you don't have to be good at dancing to enjoy it. Indeed, one of the advantages of dancing is that most people start having fun immediately. Lots of fun. I've observed this countless times at my Fred Astaire studios. Students become elated after only one lesson. They derive as much enjoyment from taking their first steps as they do when, months later, they've mastered a complicated routine. And with that elation comes a change in outlook: People suddenly feel that they're capable of more than they imagined. And because of the range of choices—smooth dances like the waltz being very easy on the body—this also is true of those whose physical condition is less than optimal.

One of my students had suffered a heart attack. Her doctor recommended ballroom dancing as a form of rehabilitation. Even though she was fairly young, in her late 40s, when she arrived for her first lesson, she couldn't walk more than a few steps without stopping to catch her breath. But soon she got stronger, she started losing weight, and her body became more toned. Within a year, this woman was able to perform all of the primary ballroom dances, including the Latin numbers, which are the most demanding. She competed and she appeared in public showcases. Eventually, she purchased a studio of her own, just so she could dance whenever and however long she wished. It's no exaggeration to say that dancing saved her life—and that it's keeping her alive today. By the way, the former heart patient is now in her 60s.

Dancing also broadens the social horizons of students by introducing them to other men and women as well as giving them an opportunity, within a safe environment, to improve their social skills. Taking dance lessons is a virtually stress-free way to interact with new people. You're not drinking at a bar. You're not on the make. You're just having a good time, while becoming more physically fit as well as more confident—in short, more appealing. Across the country, Fred Astaire studios host weekly parties for students. The purpose of the gatherings is to provide a transitional stage between the studio lesson, where students dance with instructors and everything is under the instructor's control, and the nightclub, where students might dance with complete strangers and anything can happen. And this is but one aspect of a much larger phenomenon that has swept across America in recent years. Amateur dance parties—private and public, small and large—are now taking place everywhere.

Perhaps the most exciting development, and certainly the one that's most relevant to the themes of this book, is the increase in couples participating in ballroom dancing. At Fred Astaire, for example, couples now represent 70 percent of all students. And couples, ranging from those who are married to those who are dating to ad hoc nonromantic partners, make up most of the new people showing up at dance clubs, social halls, and similar gatherings. Besides the sheer physical and psychological joy ballroom dancing offers, the increase in popularity is due, I'm convinced, to an old-school hunger: We'd all like a little more romance in our lives. And that's exactly what awaits us on the dance floor. For a short time, we are relieved of our parental, occupational, and other serious responsibilities. We dress up in elegant suits and beautiful dresses. Men become princes, women princesses. This temporary fantasyland is, of course, what sold me on ballroom dancing in the first place. Becoming the belle of the ball, if only briefly, was immensely seductive. It still is. And despite the changes that have taken place in our views of male and female roles, I believe most of us still want a refuge, a place apart from the pressures and difficulties of everyday existence, where for an hour, an evening, maybe a weekend, men and women can celebrate each other and be the heroes of their own lives.

I've seen couples take up golf, tennis, jogging, and various other physical activities in an attempt to breathe new life into their relationships. But ballroom dancing is unique in that it brings two people into close contact. It's a very intimate activity. To dance well, the man and woman must look at each other, must engage each other, must pay attention to each other's moods and movements, and, of course, they must touch each other. They reconnect in ways that wouldn't happen otherwise. Add this to all the other benefits of ballroom dancing and it's no wonder that some couples rekindle their romance on the dance floor, while others discover it there for the first time.

Regardless of whether you're married, single, or somewhere in between, as you're dancing through life don't forget to set aside some time to actually dance. It's a small pleasure with a big payoff.

I began the book with an invitation: *Take my hand as I take you on a tour of the dance floor.* Since then we've been engaged in a dance of our own making, during which, forgive me, I've been doing all the talking. I can't help but wonder what you've been thinking as I've chattered on about everything under the sun.

Be that as it may, our dance now comes to an end, as all dances must. But other dances await us, on other dance floors, with other partners. The whole dance of life awaits us. As we say farewell, I have one final wish: that you always look forward, that you give your all to every step you take.

> *Always look forward. Give your all to every step you take.*

FOURTEEN

Reprise: Putting Your Best Foot Forward

Set my spirit free. Set my body free.
—ARCADE FIRE

*P*ractice won't make you perfect. Nothing can do that. But practice will increase the likelihood that you'll find fulfillment because it's the only way to discover what's possible for you. To assist you as you dance through life, I've gathered together the major concepts of the book. Think of them as tips, starting points, signposts, little jolts of spiritual energy. Think of them as ideas to test against your own experience, then modify accordingly. But above all, put the ideas to work. Embody them in your day-to-day activities. Be persistent. Always look upon missteps as necessary steps to growth and well-being. Never cease practicing.

1. Prelude: The Art of Balance

The dance floor is a fantasyland where everyone lives
  happily ever after.

Dance floor rules: You must be nice. You must share. You
  must work together. You must want to grow up.

We are our relationships.

(In life) grace is to change as (in dance) balance is to
  movement.

Living is an art, not a science.

2. First Steps

Persistence is a form of beauty.

Be gentle with yourself.

Give yourself permission to begin again—and again
  and again.

Smart people ask for help.

Give as you want to get.

We're in this together.

To keep trying is to succeed.

Life is a contact sport.

Give yourself credit for each step you take, no matter
  how small.

Success begets success.

Protect yourself by conserving your energy.

Choose your partners on the basis of who's most likely to
  help you maintain or increase your energy level.

Life is movement. Life is change. Life is renewal.

3. Silencing the Inner Critic

It's our natural state to be motivated and to want new experience.

The inner critic wastes energy you need for growth.

The inner critic wants you to turn your back on life.

You can never please the inner critic.

If you're not willing to risk falling, you won't learn to walk.

When you ignore the inner critic, you affirm life.

Surround yourself with people who won't let you be defeated by your own weaknesses.

People with a high level of self-respect know when to walk away from the destructive behavior of others.

It's difficult to get close to others without everyone getting bruised.

Everyone needs approval.

Find new, healthier ways to meet your need for approval.

Personal growth always causes discomfort.

Make a habit of thinking positively.

Don't think about it, just do it.

Rigid thinking makes people desperate.

4. Dance of Desire

Desire is the energy that moves us forward and outward— toward life and the living.

Goals provide direction.

Short-term goals are specific and highly doable.

Ideas are tools.

Select the right tools for the job.

Short-term goals should serve long-term goals.

Conviction is needed for a full life.

Ideas that work are good ideas.

Create a new self-fulfilling prophecy by cultivating a more positive self-image.

Take a stand.

Because daily circumstances shift, short-term goals require constant adjustment.

Living with conviction creates energy.

Without grace and generosity, desire leads to greed, obsession, addiction, and violence.

Help create a climate in which living with conviction is encouraged.

5. Two Left Feet

Just as everyone can learn to dance, everyone can also learn to live well.

You needn't be perfect to lead a fullfilling life.

Striving for perfection causes psychological damage, but striving for wholeness brings fulfillment.

Your task as a human being is to fill up your life space, to use the whole dance floor.

Pretending you're not fearful makes you a slave to fear.

Fear can be useful, by protecting us from real harm.

Admitting fear is liberating.

To reduce the power of negative emotions, create your own cheering section.

Like all habitual emotions, habitual fear is fear that's out of sync with circumstance.

Personal growth depends as much on unlearning bad
   habits as it does on learning good ones.
Set aside some time each day to do nothing—and to do it
   well.
Shrug off the missteps and keep moving, always
   moving.
Use attention to develop intention.
By avoiding pain, you also risk avoiding joy.
Some problems will continue to present themselves until
   we learn what they have to teach us.
It's far better to dance with two left feet than not to dance
   at all.

6. Energy in Motion

The essence of dance is energy.
Motion alters the mind.
Energy is also the essence of life.
Surrender to the dance.
To gain mastery of anything new, you must first own up
   to incompetence, ignorance.
Dancing is pure joy.
Dance works wonders for the whole human being.
Choose a physical activity you truly enjoy.
Calm the mind by calming the body.
Step over the threshold from embarrassment to
   fulfillment.
To flow with the Flow requires presence and a keen sense
   of timing.
Be present as you move from moment to moment.

7. Dancing Solo

When each partner achieves balance as an individual, the overall partnership is more likely to be balanced.

The better you are at dancing solo, the better prepared you'll be for dancing with a partner.

We need the company of other human beings in order to grow and be fulfilled.

Solo dancing can be just as fulfilling as dancing with a partner.

Solo dancing requires as much practice and persistence as any other kind of dance.

Increase your chances of finding a partner in the dance of life by becoming the best possible solo dancer.

Certain things come to us only when we cease striving for them, especially when our striving is a cover for resistance.

Making peace with solitude is a task all of us face.

Being human is a lifelong practice, a never-ending learning process.

During solo dancing, the dance itself will dictate its own rhythms, its own length. Don't accept artificial time frames.

While you search in vain for your ideal mate within your ideal time frame, you're missing real opportunities for fulfillment.

When you're dancing solo, choose a dance floor where lots of other people are dancing as well.

Those who are passionate about life are the most likely to arouse passion in others.

*Give yourself to the role you're playing now. Dance as if
 there's no tomorrow.*

The key to fulfillment as a solo dancer is generosity.

8. Duets

For romance to last, you need much more than romance.

*The less a relationship is based on choice, the more
 potential there is for harm being done.*

*Cultivate romantic relationships in which both partners
 achieve fulfillment—separately and together.*

Generosity is the most powerful force in the universe.

Start where you are.

*Sometimes dissatisfaction with others reflects dissatisfaction
 with oneself.*

*Nothing is more nourishing to the human spirit than the
 approval of those we care about most.*

Look for the gold in people, then help it grow.

*From time to time, all couples will find themselves out
 of sync.*

Surrender to romance.

*Cooperation and continual renewal are necessary for
 romance to last.*

Love is always a work in progress.

Instead of throwing stones, help carry the weight.

Loving well, like living well, comes only after lots of practice.

*In a strong partnership, each person is capable of standing
 on his or her own two feet.*

*Encouraging independence should be a long-term goal in
 relationships between equals.*

Mutual generosity is a continual exchange of energy that nurtures each partner while strengthening the partnership itself.

Each partner in a romantic relationship must possess both the ability to lead and a willingness to follow.

9. The Dance of Life

Couples need time apart from the world to practice being a couple.

Anything that diverts or depletes energy prevents fulfillment.

In a healthy couple, the give and take of energy produces creative tension.

To learn timing requires practice and persistence and still more practice.

No one person can satisfy all your relationship needs.

The only way to grow is by letting go.

Like dance, life is relationship in motion.

Your primary relationship is always part of a complex, interdependent web of relationships.

Always travel down the line of dance.

In life, the only way to stay on course is be alert to change and, when the time is right, to be willing to change.

Arrogance brings destruction. Humility brings delight.

You achieve fulfillment by doing, and doing again, and if that doesn't work, doing it a different way.

The most fruitful long-term goals concern character— who you are and what you can become.

What you resist will persist.

Respect is wisdom in action.

Find your element—the social settings in which you're most likely to flourish.

If you think you've exhausted what the dance of life has to offer, you've done nothing more than exhaust your own imagination.

Don't waste your energy on the small stuff, because the big stuff is coming.

Generosity is gratitude in action.

10. Taking the Lead

Everyone needs healthy dependent relationships.

In dependent relationships, the person who leads bears more responsibility, sometimes a great deal more.

Setting only short-term goals is the same as wandering aimlessly.

Responsiveness is the soul of responsibility.

Responsiveness leads to right action.

In healthy dependent relationships, the person who leads tends to give more energy than she receives.

To take the lead is not to dominate or possess but to guide and encourage.

The long-term goal of healthy dependent relationships is to nurture independence.

Dependent relationships become unhealthy when they needlessly prolong dependency.

Give those who depend upon you permission to be themselves.

Make a habit of making others feel worthy, capable.

*Leading is a skill like any other. Mistakes are inevitable—
total mastery, impossible.*

*Encourage your children to be what they want to be rather
than impose your expectations, your preset ideas of
what they should be.*

*Every child's path to personal fulfillment, to becoming a
whole individual, is unique.*

*Never question a dependent's commitment to growth
merely because his or her style of expression differs
from yours.*

*To foster independence in your children, you must hold
them more and more accountable for their own
behavior.*

*The key to being an effective parent is knowing where to
draw the line between your responsibility and your
child's accountability.*

*Always try to do the right thing because your children are
much more likely to do as you do than do as you say.*

*The best way to nurture independence is to model the
right approach to difficulty and disappointment.*

*If you're leading in the dance of life, always model
constructive behavior but never identify with the
destructive behavior of those who are following.*

*Take responsibility for the relationship while holding your
partner—and yourself—accountable for individual
behavior.*

*The final and most valuable gift you can give to your
children is to no longer treat them as children.*

11. Dance of Departure

Every farewell is a reminder that nothing lasts forever.

Cultivate a positive attitude precisely because you can't always get what you want.

Desire always comes at a cost.

One key to fulfillment is living with grace and generosity despite not always getting what we want.

Everyone must come to terms with the sense of finality that accompanies the loss of a loved one.

Coming to terms with loss means learning how to feel at home in the world again.

After a major loss, it's okay to leave the dance floor for a while.

Although grief makes you feel like you're dying, it won't kill you.

When we lose someone we love, we also lose the relationship we enjoyed with that person.

Happiness comes as an extra benefit of pursuing wholeness and fulfillment.

If you understand and respect the give-and-take of life, losing what you love won't knock you off-balance.

Learn to read the currents of life, then learn to make the currents of life work for you.

We need many different kinds of relationships to become fully realized human beings.

Bringing each moment to fulfillment is what matters most.

Nothing is more important than how you use your energies in the time you're allowed on the dance floor of life.

12. Back on the Dance Floor

*Everything worthwhile in life requires sacrifice, and
sacrifice is painful.*

*The dance of desire and the dance of departure are two
stages of the same dance. You can't have one without
the other.*

*Positive thinking is thinking that leads to action, that gets
you moving again.*

*Just as desire leads to departure, so does departure lead
back to desire.*

*Shifting attention from the past to what's in front of you
is necessary to getting back on the dance floor.*

*Make a habit of starting over, of learning and doing new
things. This will make it easier for you to keep your
balance during times of trouble.*

*When you've been immobilized by loss, try to connect
with something larger than yourself, something that
will pull you back into the flow of life.*

*If you play multiple roles, and the roles are fulfilling, you'll
be better prepared for the loss of any one particular
role.*

*Sometimes the best cure for a broken heart is caring for
others.*

*Rediscovering the dance of life brings about
self-renewal.*

Just because you can, doesn't mean you should.

*Everything you want to do will depend on maintaining a
high level of energy.*

Focus on vitality instead of vanity.

After surviving a major loss, you have an opportunity to develop new, more constructive habits.

If you start small, adopt an experimental attitude, and persist, you can develop new habits.

Sometimes one small step in the right direction is all that's needed to develop a new habit.

The more you dance through life, the more you want to dance through life.

There is life after death—your life.

13. The Dance of Your Life

Make a habit of listing your blessings and saying a prayer of thanks every day.

Give yourself wholeheartedly to the dance of life.

Always picture yourself as an active, creative agent in the world.

Humanity is a work in progress. You are a work in progress.

Action shapes character.

Taking a stand also means standing up for what's right— freedom and justice.

For some people, personal fulfillment comes through public service.

In efforts to bring about social change, as in personal growth, the process should be as fulfilling as reaching the desired outcome.

Always look forward. Give your all to every step you take.

Appendix: Beyond this Book

Smart people ask for help. And, fortunately, plenty of help is available. The following lists are aimed at those interested in dance as well as those who want to know more about strategies for change that go beyond personal development. They are meant to be suggestive, not exhaustive. I've provided information regarding dance instruction, dance events, and related dance activities across the country. You'll also find the names of a few books that explore social, economic, and political factors that the self-help—or clinical—model of human behavior doesn't adequately address.

Dance Resources

www.fredastaire.com
This is the official site of Fred Astaire Dance Studios. On the site you can locate studios in your area; shop for instructional videos, clothing, and so on; and find out about competitions, exhibitions, and other dance events that you may wish to attend. For the uninitiated, the site also includes an online dance lesson.

fred-astaire.blogspot.com
For those of you who might be interested in joining a stimulating and rapidly growing dance community, try this site.

You also may want to check out the following sites:
www.usabda.org
This is the official site of the U.S. Amateur Ballroom Dancing Association.

dance.net

dancebeat.com

The best of the independent sources. Lists dance organizations, dance competitions, and other dance events throughout the country, as well as elsewhere in the world. Also includes ads for dance partners, dance lessons, videos, etc.

dancespirit.com

danceronline.com

dancebeatinternational.com

dancescape.com

Popular dance-related print publications include the following:

Dance Beat magazine

Dance Magazine

Dance Expression magazine

Social Change Resources

Your local bookstore stocks many worthwhile social change books. I'm going to keep it simple by listing four books that feature lots of inspirational stories about ordinary people who have worked together to address collective problems, thereby improving their neighborhoods, communities, and the country as a whole. All four are by the same author, Paul Loeb, who has been chronicling citizen activism and community engagement for the past thirty years. Each book contains numerous references to other social change books and related sources of information.

The Impossible Will Take a Little While: A Citizen's Guide to Hope in a Time of Fear (Basic Books, 2004).

Soul of a Citizen: Living with Conviction in a Cynical Time (St. Martin's Press, 1999).

Generation at the Crossroads: Apathy and Action on the American Campus (Rutgers University Press, 1994).

Hope in Hard Times: America's Peace Movement and the Reagan Era (Lexington Books, 1987).